THE ESSENTIAL G
SCOTCH WH

To
Ed Zern
Transatlantic Sportsman and Literary Critic
Who has assessed some fine malt whiskies with me
(v. Glossary p.171)

THE ESSENTIAL GUIDE TO
Scotch Whisky

MICHAEL BRANDER

illustrated by Rosamund Fowler

CANONGATE

First published in 1990 by
Canongate Publishing Ltd
16 Frederick Street
Edinburgh

British Library Cataloguing in Publication Data
Brander, Michael, *1924-*
The essential guide to Scotch whisky.
1. Scotch Whiskies
I. Title
641.252

ISBN 0-86241-301-X
Typeset by Falcon Typographic Art Ltd
Edinburgh & London

Printed and bound in Denmark
By Nørhaven A/S

Contents

Acknowledgements   vi

Foreword   vii

The Background of Scotch Whisky   9

A General Introduction to Scotch Whisky   31
    and to the Directory of Malt Whiskies

Map   42

A Directory of Malt Whiskies   45

An Almanack of Scotch Whisky   159

Glossary of Technical Terms   165

Further Reading: A Bibliography of Scotch   173

Acknowledgements

This is the fourth book I have written on various aspects of Scotch Whisky, starting with a General History in 1974, a Guide to Scotch Whisky in 1975 and a short Introduction to Scotch Whisky in 1982. Canongate have now asked me to combine the essentials of these three books, all now out of print, in a brief but comprehensive introduction to the malt whiskies of Scotland, with a glance at the background of Scotch Whisky. As before I must place on record my thanks to very many people throughout the Scotch whisky industry for their ready and willing assistance. It is invidious to single out individuals or groups and many prefer not to be mentioned, understandably enough, but I must put on record how very helpful everyone has been whom I have approached from the Scotch Whisky Association downwards. In particular I would like to thank the many distillers and distillery workers who have always been helpful and pleasant to meet. My thanks for help in finding a way through the maze of recent takeovers and closures are due especially to Hector MacLennan at the Dumbarton office of Allied Distillers, Bill Burgess at William Teachers, Ross Gunn, Mark Lawson and Neil Shaw at Seagram Distillers, Moyra Peffer at Whyte & Mackay, Jeremy Gilbert at Justerini & Brooks, Dr J. W. Hyatt and Carol Taylor at United Distillers, Sylvia Corrieri at Long John International, George Melville and Mrs McEwan at the Scotch Whisky Heritage Centre and many others. Any opinions expressed are entirely my own and for any faults, omissions or mistakes I am entirely responsible.

Foreword

This is intended as a guide to anyone interested in Scotch whisky. There is a brief introduction to the origins of Scotch from the earliest days to the present, showing how the drink is essentially a product of Scotland's barley, water and peat as well as the inherited skills of the distillers which have passed down the centuries. The years when Scotch whisky was produced illegally because of crushing taxation are also briefly outlined. Then came the boom years of the last century when Scotch whisky was first sold all round the world. These were followed by the lean years of the two world wars until finally the post 1945 period was reached. Michael Brander shows how foreign investment has not always been a good thing and how successive governments have damaged Scotland's greatest industry. He also shows how patent-still grain whisky is made and how this differs crucially from pot-still malt distilling. He then delineates the art of the blender and from that indicates how Scotch whisky, whether blended or malt, should be drunk. After this brief but illuminating introduction, in the major part of the book he goes through Scotland's malt distilleries alphabetically, indicating their whereabouts, their background, their present owners and the quality of their product. Even those who think they know their Scotch whisky will find something of value in these pages and for those who wish to learn about Scotch whisky here, devoid of frills, but with all that anyone needs know, is the perfect pocket introduction.

Aqua vitae

Uisge beatha

The Background of Scotch Whisky

Scotland's Heritage

Scotch whisky may only legally be distilled in Scotland. Any bottle claiming to contain Scotch whisky which is not distilled in Scotland from Very Old Black and White Horses made in Chile to Finest Rising Sun Scotch Whisky or Whisaki made in Tokyo, are illegal imitations and the makers may be prosecuted. Scotch whisky has been made in Scotland for centuries, but regrettably the majority of Scots themselves know remarkably little about it, or about the art of distilling it. This is a part of the national heritage about which there is still a widespread and lamentable ignorance, despite efforts during the 1980s to remedy this from the opening of distilleries as tourist attractions, to the publication of numerous books on the subject and the opening of the Scotch Whisky Heritage Centre in Edinburgh. It must be appreciated, however, that Scotch whisky distilling, especially the distilling of Scotch malt whisky in pot-stills, is not just another industry, and that Scotch whisky, especially Scotch malt whisky, is not just another drink, but that both are an integral part of Scotland itself. The pure air and water, the peat and the soil of Scotland, along with the inherited skills of the distillers themselves, combine magically in the making of Scotch whisky.

Origins

The elementary fact that alcohol boils at a lower temperature than water forms the basis of all distillation. Distilling is basically nothing more than boiling fermented liquor in a container. In primitive stills the steam is led off in a long tube, or condenser, like the elongated spout of a kettle. As the steam cools it reverts to liquid again in the form of alcohol which in such a simple still would contain lethal impurities as well. Like the invention of gunpowder, distilling probably originated in the Far East where the process may have started with primitive

9

stills using bamboo and heating the juice of naturally fermented fruits.

Arrival in Britain

When the art of distilling first reached Britain is uncertain, but the making of ale from fermented malted barley, the first stage in the distilling of Scotch whisky, was known around the 6th century and possibly earlier. It has been suggested that St Patrick introduced the art of distilling to Scotland as early as the 5th century. Producing Scotch whisky from malted barley probably started a good deal later, possibly somewhere around the 11th or 12th centuries, by which time both the Scots and the Irish were undoubtedly experienced in the art of distilling spirits. It seems likely therefore that the Scots have known the art of distilling Scotch whisky for over a thousand years.

Aqua Vitae

In Europe, where fermented grapes in the shape of wine were readily available, the distillation of wine produced brandy, known as aqua vitae, the Water of Life. In Scotland where fermented barley was the basis for ale, then the national drink, it would have been natural enough to use this as the basis for distilling, although the lees of wine were probably used at first. The use of fermented barley would have produced the earliest Scotch whisky, but at first, like brandy, this was also termed aqua vitae. It is thus difficult to say with any certainty when fermented barley was first used in place of wine, since in those early days there were no records of the distilling process.

First recorded use of malted barley

The earliest known record of malted barley being used instead of wine to make aqua vitae is in the Scottish Exchequer Rolls dated 1494 and reads: "Eight bolls of malt to Friar John Cor, wherewith to make aqua vitae." As eight bolls amounts to half a ton of malt, enough to make around seventy gallons of aqua vitae, it may be safely assumed that this was by no means the first time that Friar John Cor, or his fellow Friars, had made Scotch whisky. Although Scotch whisky had probably been produced for many years in Scottish monasteries, since the spirit was generally referred to in the early days only as aqua vitae it is not possible to say when the practice first started. It is also impossible to know when the art spread beyond the confines of the monasteries to become a purely domestic pastime.

Origins of the name Whisky

It is as late as 1618 before the first mention may be found in an account of a chieftain's funeral in the Highlands of the drinking of *Uisge beatha*. This is the Gaelic for the Water of Life and the equivalent of aqua vitae. It was natural enough by degrees simply to refer to *Uisge*. Thereafter it was a very simple corruption of the Gaelic to arrive at the word Whisky.

The early distilling process

To judge by surviving illustrations the stills of the 15th and 16th centuries were primitive indeed. Although there are plenty of entries in the Exchequer Rolls to prove that the King of Scotland and his nobles were fond of whisky the spirit in those days must have been not only powerful, but also potentially lethal. Without accurate instruments for measuring quality and strength, it required great skill and practice to draw off the pure *middle cut* of the spirit and avoid the *foreshots,* or oily and poisonous higher alcohols at the start, and the later *feints* or *aftershots,* containing the lower alcohols at the end of the distilling process. During the 16th and 17th centuries the methods of distilling were steadily improved and by this time it was a normal domestic chore, but even so it was not until the 18th century that distilling became really widespread in Scotland. Although the primitive 16th century stills probably held little more than thirty or forty gallons at most, by the mid-18th century stills holding several hundred gallons were commonplace and distilling had become both a science and an art.

Proof: The measurement of quality and strength

In these early stages gauging the quality and strength of spirit distilled was very rough and ready. One of the commoner methods was to set a measure alight and note how much was left. Another was to add a measure of gunpowder. If when lit it exploded this was considered too strong and *over proof,* but conversely if difficult to light it was considered weak and *under proof.* If it burned steadily it was considered the correct strength or *proof.*

Then in 1675 Robert Boyle developed his instrument for comparing the specific gravities of liquids and 'Boyle's Bubble', although not accurate to a fine degree, was used to decide whether a spirit was below or above proof. It was over a hundred years before an improvement in this early hydrometer was introduced and even then it was erratic. Accurate gauging of proof was not achieved until 1818 when the government introduced a reliable hydrometer invented by an excise officer named Sikes. Under this spirit of proof strength at 51°F weighs 12/13ths of a similar quantity of distilled water.

The national drink

Until the Union of the Parliaments in 1707 ale, not whisky, was the national drink of Scotland. Ale was more popular by far, especially in the Lowlands and with the mass of the population, than the then relatively expensive and less widely available spirit. While ale may have been the most popular drink with the bulk of the nation the upper classes, professional men and the aristocracy, tended to drink mainly claret, then readily obtainable from France. The imposition of a tax on malt in Scotland in 1725, contrary to the terms laid down in the Act of Union, resulted initially in widespread rioting and ultimately forced the brewers to raise the price of ale to cover their costs. It soon became apparent that a comparatively simple way to avoid the tax was to distil whisky illicitly instead of making ale and a gradual change in the public taste resulted. By the end of the 18th century whisky had replaced ale as the national drink. There was also the interesting side-effect towards the end of the 18th century that the Lowland distillers, distilling legally and paying tax on their malted barley, were forced to use quantities of unmalted barley to keep their costs down. Their whisky was thus naturally inferior to that of the Highland distillers who paid no tax and distilled their whisky illicitly.

Early Lowland distillers: Haig and Stein

At least one of the names subsequently to become prominent in the Scotch whisky industry had already been noted publicly in that connection as early as the latter half of the 17th century. A farming family named Hage at Throsk near Stirling were accused of distilling whisky on the Sabbath in the year 1655 and were summoned before the Kirk Session to be rebuked for their sins, but in the end their servant lass was held to blame. From the 18th century onwards the Haigs were to become one of the leading families in the Lowlands in the developing Scotch whisky industry there and went on, of course, to become one of the best known names in Scotch whisky right up to the present day. They intermarried with the Steins another well-known Lowland distilling family of the late 18th and early 19th centuries. By the last quarter of the 18th century Robert and John Haig at Leith and James and John Stein at Clackmannan were using stills of over a thousand gallons capacity. To avoid the malt tax they used potatoes, turnips and other roots, or oats and wheat for distilling, using only small quantities of malted barley to aid the fermenting process. Although this spirit was much inferior to that produced from malted barley there was a great demand for the product in the highly populated Lowlands and they also exported it to England where it was refined into gin, even engaging in a deliberate trade war with the gin distillers in England.

Penal taxation: causes and effects

This competition from Scotland roused the anger of the powerful gin distillers' lobby in England. As a result of their pressures the government was persuaded to intro-duce what amounted to punitive taxation against the Scottish whisky distillers, basing this initially on the mis-taken belief that a still could only be worked once in 24 hours. Ever increasing taxation from 1784 onwards and throughout the war with France led to ever increasing evasion and also to desperate measures to stay within the law. Ingenious Scottish distillers successfully distilled as much as eighty gallons of whisky in three and a half minutes, but naturally this tended to damage both the stills and the standard of whisky produced. The Haigs managed to survive, but the Steins, who had engaged in a cut-throat war with the southern distillers were forced into bankruptcy. As taxation still continued to rise under pressure from the English distillers many Scots distillers were literally forced to turn to illegal distilling to survive.

The Highland Line

From the 1770s onwards distilling became more and more widespread in the Highlands, but still on a much smaller scale than in the Lowlands. One of the seemingly minor pieces of legislation introduced in 1784 to simplify the taxation laws was the introduction of what became known as the Highland Line, a somewhat arbitrary line running roughly from Glasgow to Dundee. Anything north of this line was regarded as Highland and taxed at a much lesser degree than in the Lowlands. Steadily increasing taxation on whisky from 1784, led to more and more illicit distilling in the Highlands where, unlike the Lowlands, it was still very much more a cottage industry practiced on every croft and small farm to make ends meet. Without the income from distilling whisky it would have been impossible for the average highland tenant farmer of this period to pay his rent.

The shape of the still

In the early days the stills varied very greatly in size and shape but by the end of the 18th century they had mostly standardised into something approaching the modern form, which evolved largely because of the need to distil at a great speed to beat the taxation system. Naturally enough the illicit stills were nothing like as elaborate as those which were legally taxed. By the late 18th century, however, there were several master coppersmiths openly advertising their wares in Inverness under the sign of a whisky still.

An illicit still

A simple illicit still might be made from a cauldron with a cover and a spout fitted tightly in place with tow, like a lid. The spout would lead off to a coil, or worm, a spiral of copper tubing, often enclosed in a barrel with cold water from a nearby burn flowing through it to hasten the cooling process. With the cooling came the condensation of the spirit. Such primitive stills could be readily moved and were usually sited in a convenient cave, or hollow, on a hillside close to a burn supplying readily available water.

The distilling process

Sufficient sacks of barley would be steeped in the burn for around three days before being spread out to germinate in the cave, or a convenient barn. The germinating barley had to be turned every day for some ten days before being dried over a peat fire to halt the germination when it was felt to have reached the right stage. This malted barley was then placed in a mash tun, generally a large barrel, and water was poured over it. This was then stirred every few hours until the resulting mixture was drained off into another barrel and the process repeated. The liquor resulting from this process was and still is known as wort and the product of these two soakings of the grain would then be mixed together in a larger barrel and yeast would be added to them to assist in the fermentation. The resulting liquid, known as low wash, would then be heated and put through the still and became transformed into low wines. The still had then to be thoroughly cleaned before the low wines were put through it again, with the end result finally becoming malt whisky. This method, greatly refined and using two separate pot stills, is more or less how malt whisky is produced today.

The Act of 1823

In 1823 after a Board of Trade Commission had reported on the facts to Parliament a reforming Act to eliminate illegal distilling was introduced with the support of the Duke of Gordon. A flat rate of £10 was introduced on all stills of forty gallons upwards and a duty of 2s 3d placed on each gallon of spirits distilled. Encouraged by the Duke of Gordon, one of the first to take advantage of the new act was George Smith in Glenlivet, despite threats from his neighbours to burn down his distillery.

The effect of The Act of 1823

The immediate result was that within two years the amount of tax-paid whisky had increased from two million to six million gallons annually. The long term effect was to change what had amounted to little more than a cottage craft into a considerable industry which by the end of the century was to become one of Scotland's principal assets. The results of too high taxation on the industry are something that should still be borne in mind and it may be argued that this stage has already been reached and passed with as dire effects on the industry today as in 1820.

Pot-still distilling: first stage

The method of producing malt whisky by pot still distillation was by this time well developed. The best available Scottish barley was transported to the distillery by pack-horse, cart or boats, where it was placed in large steeps, or tanks. Water was then poured over and it was left for around 48 hours to soak thoroughly. It was then spread on the floor of the malting shed with its characteristic Chinese pagoda-like roof ventilators and was left for something like eight days to reach the right stage of germination. To regulate the degree of heat in the malting barley it was turned at regular intervals. When the required state of germination had been reached the starch in the barley had all by this time been transformed into sugar. It was then heated in a kiln over peat fires to check the germination thus imparting a peaty smokey flavour to the whisky.

Second stage

The malted grain was then bruised in the mill before being put into the mash tun where heated water was added and the mixture stirred. The peaty water would add its own flavour and with added yeast the mixture, now known as wort, fermented in special fermenting vats for some three days during which the sugar was converted into alcohol. The resulting wash was then led into the wash still, standing beside the spirit still.

The wash still and the spirit still

In any malt whisky distillery today the wash still and spirit still may be seen standing side by side, at first sight apparently identical to each other. The wash in the wash still is heated to boiling point when the alcohol rises through the worm, or coil, in its cold water jacket. It is then discharged as low wines directly into the adjacent spirit still. The same process of heating the low wines to boiling point then takes place and the same process ensues but this time the spirit produced is malt whisky. This in turn is then placed in oak barrels, preferably casks in which sherry had been kept, and is aged for a minimum of three, but generally nearer eight to ten years, or sometimes as much as twelve, fifteen or more, before becoming accepted as the finest drink that any country could produce.

Unique to Scotland

The process of malt whisky pot-still distillation today is in essentials virtually unchanged from the first quarter of the 19th century. The whiskies themselves, even when produced in almost identical areas, using apparently identical pot stills and even when using the same water supply are never the same. Despite all efforts to duplicate the process in other countries the distilling of Scotch malt whisky remains unique to Scotland.

The silent season

During the summer months, when the burns and springs supplying the old distilleries tended to run dry, and when it often grew too warm for the malting process to be carried through successfully, distilling was abandoned for several weeks during what was termed the 'silent season'. During this period distillery maintenance and repairs were usually carried out. As the autumn set in distilling would then start again. Some distilleries even today have a silent season when repairs are carried out and distilling is discontinued.

The introduction of the continuous patent-still

In 1828 a new invention revolutionised the whisky industry when Robert Stein, one of the Lowland whisky distilling family, produced the first continuous patent still. This distilled in one continuous process, without the double distillation required in pot-still distillation. Only four years later in 1832 Aeneas Coffey, an ex-Inspector General of Excise in Ireland, patented a simpler continuous still which became known as the Coffey still and quickly superseded Stein's more cumbersome invention.

The patent-still

The continuous still is basically little more than two 40 feet high copper columns side by side, linked by a junction pipe at the top. These are known as the analyser and rectifier and each column consists of a number of horizontal compartments containing perforated copper plates. A jet of steam is passed through these columns and the wash is pumped into the still through a pipe coiled around the length of the rectifier from the top downwards, both cooling the latter and also heating the wash before it enters the top of the analyser column. On entering the analyser column the heated wash encounters an upwards pressure of steam surging through the perforated chambers. Since alcohol boils and evaporates at lower temperatures than water the alcohol separates from the wash as it descends chamber by chamber through the perforated plates. The alcohol then rises with the steam and entering the base of the rectifier column condenses on the perforated plates of each chamber. The purest alcohol rises to the top and the heavier higher alcohols and lower alcohols condense at lower levels since they have lower boiling points and are drawn off for re-distilling. The end product of this method of distilling is almost pure alcohol and since it is a continuous process can be continued as long as wash is available to put through the still.

Grain Whisky

The whisky produced by this process became known as patent-still, or grain, whisky, to differentiate it from the malt whisky produced by the malt whisky distillers, using the slower traditional method requiring two pot stills. The grain whisky distillers were naturally able to produce far greater quantities of their whisky than the malt whisky distillers and there was keen rivalry between the two, with the slower pot-still distillers inevitably the losers. Since almost all the new patent stills were situated convenient to the large centres of population in the Lowlands there was also an element of the familiar antagonism between Highlander and Lowlander which is even today to be found not far below the surface.

The merchants

The middle-men who sold the whisky in the mid-19th century, many of whom at this stage were little more than family grocers, began to grow in importance with the growth of the Scotch whisky industry itself. Like middle-men in many other industries they reaped considerable profits and their power developed to the stage where they could dictate their own terms to the whisky distillers, more especially the small pot-still malt whisky producers. Being individualists to a man the latter especially were very slow to combine and while the rest of the Scotch whisky industry gradually began to merge and consolidate they were the last to see the advantages of union.

Whisky at this stage

The patent-still, or grain, whisky was made from any grain, oats, rye, or maize, crushed and boiled to break up the starch. During the mashing process a little malted barley would be added then fermentation on a large scale would take place. The result was that it was not only produced in much larger quantities, but it was much quicker, cheaper and easier to produce than the slow twice distilled, pot-still distillation methods. Furthermore it was generally much more even, being more or less tasteless pure spirit. The malt distillers, seldom operating with more than two or four stills and relying largely on the skill of the individual still-man supervising the distilling process, often produced very varying single malt whiskies, (i.e. malt whisky from one distillery unmixed with any other) which not only tasted very strong to southern palates, but also varied considerably with each distilling. To the discerning the differences might be both interesting and desirable, but they did not make it easy to sell. It was only when grain whisky was added to single malt whiskies to make a standardised blend that was smoother and more acceptable to southern palates that sales began to rise.

Blended Whisky

From the 1850s onwards, especially, the growth of the Scotch whisky industry was dramatic. It was a merchant, Andrew Usher & Co., agent for The Glenlivet malt whisky who is credited with first introducing blended whisky in 1853. The term blended whisky, was at first used to describe a mixture of malt whiskies, now known as vatted malts, but in time came to be used as today to describe the addition of malt whisky to grain whisky, making the blended whiskies we know today. At the time it is doubtful if the full significance of this innovation was appreciated, but inevitably it led to cut-throat competition in the industry as the trade expanded over the second half of the 19th century. By that time, however, the industry had shed its old illicit image and was highly organised with a Customs man then present in each distillery who had charge of a set of keys providing sole access to the Spirit still and bonded store where the whisky produced was kept to mature.

The early cartels

The earliest 'trade arrangement', as it was euphemistically termed, was entered into in 1856 by six firms of distillers. In the 1860s the cartel was re-formed and in 1877 the firms concerned decided to merge. They were: John Bald & Co., Carsebridge Distillery, Alloa; John Haig & Co., Cameron Bridge Distillery, Fife; Macfarlane & Co., Port Dundas Distillery, Glasgow; MacNab Bros & Co., Glenochil Distillery, Menstrie; Robert Mowbray, Cambus Distillery, Alloa; Stewart & Co., Kirkliston Distillery, Lothian. Together they formed The Distillers Company Limited, based in Edinburgh, which steadily developed by merger and take-overs to become the leading force in the industry for the best part of a hundred years, attaining its greatest period of strength before and after the 1939-45 War.

The brand names

From around 1853 to the 1870s the blended whiskies sold in the south were often little more than grain whisky with a minimal amount of malt, pot-still, whisky added. Nevertheless a number of very able reputable merchants and distillers began to emerge producing recognised standard whiskies with specific brand names. With consummate salesmanship they spread the sales of Scotch not only throughout England but onto the continent and throughout the British Empire and elsewhere in the civilised world. As a result of their efforts blended whisky came to be recognised throughout the world as the product of Scotland.

Phylloxera vastatrix and 'The Big Five'

The effects of *Phylloxera vastatrix*, a fatal disease which attacked the roots of the vines, on the French wine and, hence also the brandy, producers had been disastrous in the 1870s and '80s and the producers of Scotch whisky were not long in seizing their opportunity. Scotch whisky soon came to fill the gap in the market. Famous names such as James Buchanan's 'Black and White', Peter Mackie's 'White Horse', Alexander Walker's 'Johnnie Walker', The Dewar brothers, John and Tommy, John Haig and others had begun to dominate the industry. These, however, were widely known as 'The Big Five', who were all recognised and celebrated salesmen and founders of famous brand names of various blended whiskies sold widely throughout the world and also widely advertised. The flamboyant salesmanship of Tommy Dewar endeared him to the Press and the public, even if it was his brother John who was the steadying influence. James Buchanan's tall handsome figure and considerable presence made him a powerful personality in any company. Peter Mackie too was a man who naturally hit the headlines and influenced the industry. These were amongst the men who dominated the whisky industry during the boom years of the 1880's and 90's. Although the Distillers Company Limited was the growing power behind the scenes, which ultimately under the superb direction of William Ross was to take them all over, they were the names the public chiefly associated with the Scotch whisky industry at this time and to a large extent they were also responsible for its rapid growth.

Malt Whisky distillers

This is not to say that the pot-still malt whisky distillers were unable to survive. There were still many small malt whisky distillers and despite the strong and powerful Lowland grain distillers and the power of the merchants they managed to keep going for there were still considerable local sales within Scotland itself, as well as regular sales to discriminating merchants and blenders who knew what they required. At this stage there were several clear groupings of pot-still malt whisky distillers. There were basically the Highland distillers, notably in Speyside based mainly round the Central Highland Speyside area, and the Lowland distillers below the Highland Line to be found as far south as Dumfriesshire and East Lothian. There were also those on the Islands, mainly on the west coast, particularly on Islay. There were in addition 34 concentrated in and around the west coast town of Campbeltown, then known as the malt whisky capital of Scotland. Most of these area groupings, with the notable exception of Campbeltown, remain in existence today.

The end of the Scotch Whisky boom

Although by the 1890s most of the big brand names we know today such as 'Black & White', 'Haig', 'Queen Anne', 'Johnnie Walker' and 'Vat 69' to name only a few, were selling well throughout the world there were also many dubious fly-by-night firms cashing in on the boom by selling whisky of a very low standard at inflated prices. One of the more flamboyant and dubious firms blending and selling their own whisky at this time were Pattison's Ltd, controlled by two brothers, Robert and Walter Pattison, who had started as dairy wholesalers and graduated to dispensing whisky because they felt there was more profit in that than in selling watered milk. They found they could buy cheap grain whisky at under a shilling a gallon and by adding a minute quantity of malt whisky could sell it at 8s 6d a gallon, describing it as 'Finest Glenlivet'. One of their more bizarre attempts at advertising included distributing to their retailers some 500 parrots which were allegedly trained to say 'Drink Pattison's Whisky'. Despite, or because of, such sales methods they went bankrupt in 1898 to the then almost unheard of sum of £82,000. Investigation soon revealed fraud on a large scale as well as making public the more deplorable methods of blending used by the disreputable end of the whisky industry. Their trial, combined with the outbreak of the Boer War, brought the whisky boom to an abrupt end. It also brought before the public attention for the first time the argument of the pot-still whisky distillers that grain whisky was not really Scotch whisky.

The Islington Borough Council

In 1906 the Islington Borough Council took a local publican to court for selling grain whisky alleging that this was 'not of the nature, substance and quality demanded by the purchaser.' The Distillers Company Limited failed to take the case seriously and the result seemed a resounding triumph for the pot-still malt distillers when it was held that 'whisky should consist of a spirit distilled in a pot-still derived from malted barley . . .'

The Royal Commission of 1909

Although at first hailing this legal decision as a resounding victory, the malt whisky distillers quickly realised that the enormously wealthy Lowland distillers would simply distil very cheap Lowland malts and use them instead of their Highland malts to produce blended whisky. Both sides therefore asked for a Royal Commission to decide the issue and after eighteen months, in 1909, the Commission very sensibly concluded that' whiskey (the current spelling of the period) is a spirit obtained by the distillation of a mash of cereal grains saccharified by the diastase of the malt; that 'Scotch whiskey' is whiskey, as above defined, distilled in Scotland . . .' This definition of Scotch whisky was finally incorporated in Statute Law (as late as 1952) and is thus accepted by every government throughout the world. Because of this ruling Scotch whisky may not be distilled in any other country in the world.

Increasing taxation
The first increase in taxation for forty years took place in 1900 when it was raised to eleven shillings from the ten shillings per gallon set by Gladstone in 1860. In 1909, taking full advantage of the split in the industry resulting from the Royal Commission's findings David Lloyd George, then Chancellor of the Exchequer and a lifelong rabid teetotaller, raised the tax per proof gallon by a further 3s 9d to 14s 9d. Without united opposition from within the industry the increase was passed, a foretaste of things to come and a warning to both distillers and merchants of the dangers of lacking unanimity.

The Scottish Malt Distillers Limited
Just before the outbreak of the 1914-18 War the Distillers Company Limited, already the most powerful moving force in the industry, amalgamated five Lowland Malt Whisky distillers into a group called the Scottish Malt Distillers Limited. Inevitably many of the malt whisky distilleries which found themselves unable to survive the rigours of the war years were absorbed into this growing DCL subsidiary.

The effects of the 1914-18 War
The DCL was large enough to survive the war years and even prosper under the able directorship of its outstanding managing director, William Ross. Its patent still distilleries were employed in producing industrial alcohol for war-time use. During the entire war the DCL continued to expand, through mergers, amalgamations and take-overs. In 1917 the government restricted distilling solely to producing industrial alcohol. The Central Liquor Control Board also decreed that all spirits should be diluted to 50 under proof or 70% proof. The industry responded

by forming the Whisky Association, a central body to defend the interests of all distillers, both patent-still and pot-still, blenders, merchants and exporters. In spite of this the price of whisky rose from 20s to 80s owing to lack of controls.

From 1918-20

In 1918 seeking a means of financing the enormous costs of the war the government more than doubled the tax per proof gallon of whisky from 14s 9d to 30s, a total rise of 15s 5d. This naturally produced more revenue in the short term and encouraged the Chancellor of the Exchequer to add a further 20s in 1919 making the total tax a matter of 50s per proof gallon, more than trebling the level of taxation within three years. In 1920 the government went even further and raised the tax by 22s 6d to 72s 6d per proof gallon, thus making a fivefold increase within three years, the sort of burden which would inevitably be a strain on any industry, not least one attempting to recover from the effects of a major war.

Prohibition

The year 1920 also saw the introduction of Prohibition in the United States of America. Pot-still malt distilling had only been permitted to start again in 1919 with the distillers looking forward to a minor boom in post-war years. The effects of the high taxation and Prohibition caused a major depression in the industry instead and this lasted throughout the 1920s until the end of Prohibition in 1932, by which time that imprudent if well intentioned experiment had been totally discredited. During this period of depression in the industry only the DCL empire was sufficiently strong and powerful to continue to expand. Four of the 'Big Five', Haig, Johnny Walker, Buchanan and Dewar, had already been amalgamated, and finally in 1927, but only after his death, Sir Peter Mackie's White Horse Distillers, were also absorbed into the DCL. The DCL was by then the only company in the whole industry sufficiently powerful to continue to open up new fields abroad, but even so it was mainly by diversification that it survived successfully, especially after the Great Depression of 1930.

The Pot-Still Malt Distillers Association

In 1926 the Pot-Still Malt Distillers Association of Scotland was formed to replace the old North of Scotland Malt Distillers Association as an all-embracing association of all Scottish Malt Whisky distillers. It is, however, indicative of how deeply the Depression had affected the industry that in 1933 the Association recommended to its members that there should be no distilling at all that year and by that time there were only fifteen distilleries operating in the whole of Scotland with several of these only operating on a part-time basis. Although the DCL then controlled 33 Highland distilleries in addition to five in Campbeltown and five in Islay most of these had merely been acquired in order to close them down. Excessive taxation and the closure of the major market of the USA had brought the industry close to total ruin.

The 1930s

From the repeal of Prohibition in 1930 to the outbreak of War in 1939 the industry began to recover. The process started gradually but speeded up as the world markets began slowly to expand. The outbreak of war was not entirely unexpected but was naturally a grave blow, as was the imposition of a further 10s tax per proof gallon in 1939 raising it to 82s 6d.

The 1939-45 War

In 1940 the duty per proof gallon was raised by 15s to 97s 6d. Distilling was restricted in the same year and prohibited altogether in 1941 until 1945. This did not prevent the tax being raised again in 1942 by a further 40s to 137s 6d and yet once more in 1943 by a further 20s to 157s 6d. From 1945 onwards distilling on a small scale was permitted for pot-still malt whisky distillers only, to earn much-needed dollar currency.

The Scotch Whisky Association

In 1942, recalling their experiences after the 1914-18 War and to provide the industry with the maximum security possible, the Whisky Association was wound up and replaced by the Scotch Whisky Association. Its primary objectives were: to protect and promote the interest of the Scotch whisky trade generally both at home and abroad and to do all things and take all such measures as may be conducive or incidental to the attainment of such objects.

1945–50

Although only pot-still malt distilling had been permitted in limited quantities from 1944 onwards to earn much needed dollar currency this did not stop Hugh Dalton, Socialist Chancellor of the Exchequer in 1947 raising the tax per proof gallon by 33s 4d to 190s 10d. The following year his successor Sir Stafford Cripps added a further 20s to the tax making it £10 10s 10d per proof gallon. At the same time only licenses to distil for export were granted, yet inevitably every increase of taxation in Britain was followed by corresponding increases in taxation abroad. It might be said the government cut the throat of their goose while it laid its golden eggs and that many of the ills affecting the industry may be traced back to this period.

The 1950s

Throughout the 1950s the Scotch whisky industry, already greatly weakened by the war years and by excessive taxation, was faced with fresh competition, much of it from North America, in part at least financed by British Government subsidies. It could be claimed this was not only cutting the golden goose's throat, but chopping off its limbs and feeding them to the fox for a short-term financial return.

The 1960s

In spite of repeated warnings of the inevitable effects on the industry, throughout the 1960s successive governments continued the negative policy of raising the tax per proof gallon almost annually. The tax was increased in 1961, 1964, 1965, 1966 and 1968, by which time it was £18.85 pence per proof gallon. The industry sought to protect itself by amalgamations and forming ever larger groups.

The 1970s

During the 1970s, although a similar process continued, there were different forces at work. The British currency was decimalised in 1971. In 1973 with the introduction of Value Added Tax and the entry of Britain into the European Economic Community the duty on whisky was actually reduced for the first time since 1896. This did not deter successive governments from raising the tax per proof gallon every year from 1973 to 1977. By then the tax per proof gallon amounted to £27.09. This represented duty on a bottle of whisky at the rate of £3.16 pence. Further mergers, amalgamations and takeovers resulted during this period.

The 1980s

This steady investment of foreign capital into what had always been an intensely Scottish industry continued throughout the 1980s. This was a period of severe recession, but the damage had been done, nor did the process halt. Investment from Japan, the Far East, Europe, Canada and North America continued, taking full advantage of government subsidies. Once established such companies have not always acted with the genuine long-term, or even sometimes short-term, interests of the Scotch whisky industry - or for that matter of Scotland, or indeed Britain - at heart. Little else could be expected. To encourage foreign investment to set up in competition and even subsidising them to do so can hardly be desirable and has proved in some cases against the best interests of the industry and of the country. For instance, bulk export of Scotch whisky, especially immature stocks, by such firms, has undoubtedly damaged the industry's standing and prestige abroad. This is particularly difficult to control and is merely one of the ways in which the industry has been and may continue to be adversely affected. Along with excessive taxation this absence of overall control emphasises the lack of understanding of successive governments based in London. Control of a large part of the industry has also been transferred to London following the 1987 still sub-judice acquisition by Guinness of DCL, later merged with Arthur Bell & Sons and re-named United Distillers plc, and other parts are controlled from North America, Europe and Japan. This is a serious loss to Scotland and a disastrous situation which has been created by successive governments. It might be argued that it can only finally be cured by governmental action since the Scotch Whisky Association, although a very effective trade association, has no mandate beyond those agreed by its members amongst themselves. By introducing a greater degree of control and passing those powers to a freshly created government-backed body with the interests of the industry and of Scotland at heart the situation might still be saved. As a first step for instance each firm or corporation controlling more than say two malt whisky distilleries might by law be forced to base its headquarters in Scotland. The position today is a distorting mirror image of the period in 1823 when government actions had brought about a crisis in the industry and it is only by radical action such as was taken then that matters can be satisfactorily resolved.

The International Organisation of Legal Metrology

Since 1980 Britain has adopted the standard system of proof measurement of the Common Market, measuring alcohol by percentage of volume at 20° C. Sikes 70° equals IOLM 39.9% and 75° = 42.8%: 80° = 45.6%: 100° = 57.1%: 120° = 68.5%: Malt whisky may be purchased at 70° - 105° proof measured by Sikes's method. This means they vary from approximately 40% to 60% volume.

From today to 1992 and onwards

Now that we are part of the European Economic Commission they have decreed that Scotch whisky shall be recognised as Scotch whisky only if it is distilled and produced in Scotland. Furthermore it must be no less that 40% volume, since at anything less it cannot be checked that it is indeed Scotch whisky. In the coming years the industry may regain the standards which, under foreign ownership or through financial stringency, have sometimes slipped, as when control has been by accountants based overseas interested chiefly in the quickest possible returns on their investments. That is a recipe for disaster which has resulted in bankruptcies in other largely foreign controlled industries in Scotland and the UK. The industry should also cease to be seduced, as parts of it have been during the past decade or more, by these twin PR weasel-words, marketing and presentation, into change simply for the sake of change, whether it is new bottles, new labels, new colouring or new advertising. This is an industry where time-tried methods and generations of experience are all-important assets, but, although the distillery's name on the label of a malt whisky is roughly equivalent to *Appelation Controlee* and *premier cru* on a wine bottle, possibly some indication of the standard to be expected might be given beyond those at present customary. For instance, perhaps awards for ageing in the cask for 12 or more years could be introduced corresponding to *Grand Cru*, using the Gaelic adjective Mohr, meaning Great, thus creating *A Malt Whisky Mohr*.

Highland
Lowland and Island

A General Introduction to Scotch Whisky
and to
The Directory of Malt Distilleries

A foreword on Scotch Whisky
It is important to understand something of the background of Scotch whisky making, blending and the industry as a whole before examining the pot-still malt whiskies in detail. In this brief introduction it is impossible to cover every aspect of the industry, but to appreciate and savour malt whiskies to the full it is necessary to know something of each distillery itself and these are covered briefly in the pages which follow. Ideally the distiller himself should supervise each aspect of the operation from buying the barley direct from the farmer to converting it into malt on the floor of the maltings, seeing that it is carefully turned with wooden rakes on the floor of the maltings and at the right moment dried over peat fires for the mashing and distilling processes. In large modern distilleries most of these procedures will be automated and the malted barley itself may often be obtained from an outside source, but there are still important individuals in the employ of any pot-still malt distillery on whom a great deal depends.
The still-man
One such important employee is the still-man, who is responsible for the actual distilling of the whisky. He it is who decides when to start distilling. On his judgement of when the foreshots have passed and when the 'middle cut' is running much depends. Were he to start too soon or leave matters too late and allow the foreshots and after-shots to mix with the final spirit the result would not be up to standard. Much depends on him. Even in the best regulated of distilleries, however, it may sometimes happen that some foreshots or aftershots have crept into the

distilling. Then it may be that a single bottle in a case has been filled with the last of a cask to the bottom of which the evil tasting oils have sunk. Although no distiller likes to admit it such an unpleasant off-tasting bottle is sometimes found in any distillery's products, the equivalent of a corked bottle of wine, but it is a rare occurrence indeed.

The master cooper

The distiller should ideally also have a master cooper to supervise the casks in which the spirit is kept to mature. The wastage from such casks by evaporation can otherwise be considerable and add greatly to his costs. Some degree of evaporation in the cask is anyway inevitable and is known as 'the angel's share'. The choice of cask is important. American oak is the wood usually preferred. The favoured casks are old oak sherry casks, but many distilleries use reconstructed bourbon casks, which by US law may not be re-used. Such casks have proved ideal. As long ago as 1890 the practice of soaking new wooden casks with cheap dark sherry before using them was introduced. Nowadays a compound called pajarate, a sweet colouring mixture made from grape juice and used in Jerez for sherries, is diluted and swilled round new barrels to colour the wood before they are used for whisky. Too much sherry in the whisky can lead to undue sweetness, or darker colouring, or even undesirable overtones in the whisky masking the delicate flavours. Too much wood which has not previously been used for maturing sherry, or spirit, may lead to an undesirably woody taste in the whisky stored in them. Too long in the barrel may lead to either of these. If the cooper or the still-man are not doing their jobs efficiently the distillery can soon go to the wall and it is a fiercely competitive business.

Modern technology

Sadly with the advent of ever more automated systems of distilling even pot-still distilling is losing the individual touch in many cases. The still-man in places may be seen controlling the whole business in a white coat and watching the dials on a computer. Where there are several stills in one distillery the likelihood is that the contents of each will be mixed together to make up one standardised single malt whisky rather than allow the individual variations of each distilling to go through to the customer which used to make pot-still malt whiskies such an exciting business to taste and savour in the same way that each fresh crop of the vineyards produces fresh and exciting vintages. The modern craving for standardisation is a big mistake when applied to malt whiskies.

The conglomerates

When the big conglomerates take over and try to stream-line the industry with numerous stills, vast whisky vats and control by computer something inevitably goes out of the product. Sadly the foreign takeovers of pot-still malt distilleries and the big conglomerate acquisitions have gone almost unopposed because of successive govern-ments, savage taxation of the whisky industry. Fortunately there are still some shining exceptions.

The Grants

The Grants, particularly, are a resilient clan, to which I am happy to be related, and they have had and continue to have a considerable influence on distilling in Scotland. It is a name which figures largely in any history of pot-still malt whisky distilling. There are of course many others who are concerned to see that pot-still distilling of malt whisky should continue in the traditional way to produce fine and distinctive single-malts. This part of the industry is fully alive and continuing to flourish.

Blended Whisky

Blending Scotch whisky is a skilled task accomplished by experts who 'nose' their various whiskies, savouring the bouquet and making up the various proportions which form the final blend. As many as thirty, or more, malt whiskies may be used to make up a specific blend. Year after year their task is to produce exactly the same taste in their blend. The major recognised blends do not alter very perceptibly in taste over the years entirely owing to their expertise. Knowing also the particular tastes of the countries to which their blends are destined for export they can subtly alter them to match the required demand, not only for taste but also for colour and consistency.

Nosing

Unlike wine it is not possible simply to taste whisky by swilling the neat spirit round the mouth. To do so would merely be to destroy the sense of taste almost immediately. A single measure of whisky should be poured into a tulip shaped glass, although a wine glass is satisfactory for most purposes, and at 40% volume a similar quantity of pure water added. If the aroma is then smelt the expert can deduce the origins of the blend or, if a malt, details of its distilling and maturing process. When the volume is greater he will require to add more pure water accordingly. He will also always start with the less powerful and go on to the stronger more highly flavoured, since to do otherwise would be to miss the more delicate scents. These of course, would be lost if chlorinated tap water was used instead of pure water. A heavy smoker, or someone addicted to peppermints or chewing gum, or strong tasting foods like curries, or anyone with a cold, is unlikely to be able to achieve much by nosing. It is essential to keep the sense of smell and taste as acute as possible, but given practice even a heavy smoker may appreciate something of the differences between malts in this way.

Colour

The blender will also bear in mind the colour of whisky preferred by his customer. For instance the majority of States in the USA prefer a light coloured whisky, perhaps on the grounds that a large light coloured whisky does not appear any darker in the glass than a small light coloured whisky. Since whisky when distilled is almost colourless some degree of colouring is often added. Although malt whisky may acquire a certain amount of colour while it is being matured in old oak sherry casks it is an open secret that this can also be due to caramel or even sherry.

Blenders in practice will have a colour chart available to assist them and it is not a difficult matter to produce any colour that is required. So far, thank goodness, no-one has tried to market pink whisky like pink champagne, but no doubt it will not be long before this too is tried.

Grain Whisky

Fine Old Cameron Brig produced by Haig at their distillery at Glenrothes in Fife was for a long time the only pure grain whisky for sale, but others are now available, notably Invergordon. By choosing your own malt whiskies and blending them with these it is, of course, possible to make your own blended whisky. It is also possible and pleasurable to mix your own malt whiskies to achieve perfection.

D.I.Y.

The beauty of Scotch whisky is that it is perfectly possible for the discriminating drinker to make up a blend, or a mixture of malt whiskies, known as a vatted malt whisky, entirely to his own taste, if he wishes to find out whether he can improve on those produced commercially. There is little doubt that by choosing his blends shrewdly and adding a measure of malt whisky to them he can often greatly improve the blend he is drinking at least to his own satisfaction. The same is undoubtedly true of mixing malt whiskies and producing a vatted malt which is, to his particular taste, an improvement on the originals used to make up the end product. Contrasting malt whiskies by selecting three or four amongst the finest, then after nosing and savouring them, taking a little of each in differing quantities together in one glass is always exciting.

In this way nectar may be achieved, but in the nature of things it is a nectar that is constantly changing since the constituents themselves are never quite the same. Over the years, inevitably, malt whiskies change and their characters alter as the men who make them and control their destiny also change.

Drinking Scotch Whisky

How anyone drinks Scotch whisky is entirely up to them. There are cocktails made from Scotch whisky, some of which are even drinkable. Some people prefer to drown the taste of their Scotch whisky in ginger ale, or orange juice. Others always insist on drinking their Scotch, whether malt or blend, neat, on the grounds that it is already watered before sale. Certainly some tap water tastes strongly of chloride and other additives but to obtain the greatest satisfaction from a mature blend or a fine malt many people will rightly maintain that a little pure water improves the drink, probably as in 'nosing' at least an equal quantity of water at 40% volume, but remember even carbonated spring waters can alter the flavour of a fine malt whisky. It is, however, in the end a matter of individual choice and taste, for Scotch whisky in all its forms is a highly individual drink. It is the product of the country's lochs and rivers, of the barley, the peat, the labour and the centuries-old expertise of Scots. It is the very essence of Scotland itself. Drink it as you wish but above all enjoy it.

The Malt Whiskies

There are still over a hundred malt whisky distilleries to be found in Scotland. It is the malt whisky from these which provides the essential flavours of the Scotch itself, whether drunk individually, in conjunction with others as vatted malts, or as blended whisky mixed with grain, or patent-still, whisky. These malt whiskies are to the connoisseur what the *premier cru* wines are to the wine drinker. No two are alike and each separate bottling may differ from the last, although today a high degree of standardisation has been achieved. Whether this is always necessarily a good thing is another matter, but it has to be said that it does make the task of the blender easier. It is however still a matter for congratulation that each malt whisky has its own unique taste and aftermath.

Ageing and maturing

By the legal definition of Scotch whisky contained in the Scotch Whisky Act 1988, no Scotch whisky may be sold under three years old and most are in fact kept in the cask until matured for five years at least. There is usually a particular age at which it is considered that individual malt whiskies achieve their best. This may vary from five to eight years, ten or twelve, or even fifteen and upwards, although in some cases more may be lost than gained after twelve or so. Two or three years then may make a big difference. Some malt whiskies mature faster than others. Where no age is given for a malt whisky it is reasonable to assume around five or at most six. Lowland malt whiskies are generally said to be mature enough to bottle at five years. It should be added that while whisky matures and alters perceptibly while kept in a cask it is unlike wine in that it does not alter materially once bottled.

The geography of Malt Whisky

The malt whiskies are widely separated geographically but there are basically only two main divisions, Highland and Lowland, from above and below the Highland Line. There are, however, quite a number of west coast Highland and northern Highland malt whiskies as well as a large grouping round Speyside. There are also Island malt whiskies, particularly the Islay group and those from Orkney. Fortunately the products of the different regions as well as of the individual distilleries remain each as different from the next as claret from burgundy or sherry from port. It is this that makes the malt whiskies so satisfying to savour even if there may be general similarities of type amongst the various groups. The large grouping around Speyside may have certain recognisable similarities, but they also differ widely from each other and from other Highland groups. The Islay malt whiskies also have their own very recognisable characteristics, but again differ very much from each other. The two remaining Campbeltown malt whiskies still have a distinctive flavour of their own, as do those of Orkney, Highland Park and Scapa. So it is with the

Lowland malt whiskies. There is a wealth of choice for the enthusiast.

The Single Scotch Malt Whisky -
A question of definition

If you wish to be exact it is correct to refer to the product of a single pot-still malt whisky distillery in Scotland as a single Scotch malt whisky. The reason for calling it Scotch malt whisky is that, although not many people are likely to encounter their products in this country, there is a pot-still malt whisky distillery in Ireland and three or four in Japan, notably Suntory's, started in 1923. The reason for terming it single is that even if what is in the cask is the result of several distillations it is the product of a single distillery as distinct from a vatted malt whisky which is the product of several distilleries. This is, however, really being pedantic and leads to the absurdity that if you then wish to refer to the product of one distillation which has been casked as such it has to be termed a 'single-single malt.' The answer is always to refer to vatted malts as vatted malts and to refer to single Scotch malt whisky simply as malt whisky. Since even supermarket chains now produce their own vatted malts, some of which can be very good, they must, like the numerous blends, be left outside the scope of this book. There should be no confusion and it is simply a question of reading the label on the bottle with care.

The labelling

The label on malt whisky bottles, like the shape of the bottles themselves, is liable to change from time to time, but there are certain points which should remain constant. It should specify that it is a product of Scotland, and that it is a pure malt whisky, giving the area from which it is produced and the name of the distillery and the name of the malt whisky itself, if different, as a few are. The alcoholic strength at which it is sold must be noted as must the quantity in the bottle. The age should also be given, although some malt whiskies are sold with the age unspecified. If it is bottled by an independent bottler this will be specified, in which case it must be appreciated that it cannot be regarded as a true sample of the distillery's product since such bottlings are liable to alter from year to year in strength and in age. To give the year of the bottling, as with a wine, means nothing since whisky once in a bottle does not alter materially. If it is a blended whisky it should specify that it is Scotch whisky and a product of Scotland. It should also add, 'distilled, blended and bottled in Scotland.' If it is a vatted malt, probably styled *The Pride of this and that*, it may say that it is 'pure malt' and it may give an age, which, as is the case with blended whisky, must be the age of the youngest constituent, but it will not include the name of a distillery.

A question of taste

In describing taste, which is such an individual matter, it is next to impossible to be exact and what one man likes another may abhor. It may be said that every Scot is basically an east coast man or a west coast man, depending on which side of Scotland he was born. To the east coast man initially the west coast malts taste of seaweed and drains. To the west coast man the east coast malts taste of antiseptic. It is only by persevering that the east coast man will discover subtle differing flavours and the west coast man surprising delicate nuances of taste. I have tried to avoid generalities or vague descriptions such as nutty, which may be coconut or hazelnut or peanut or whatever, but describing what amounts to mere sensations is at times a near impossibility. Poetic flights of fancy suggesting for instance a peppermint flavour to a whisky are to my mind unhelpful and downright impossible unless it is adulterated. As far as possible I have tried to indicate the taste as plainly as possible, but it is up to everyone to make up their own minds, that is half the pleasure of the drink.

A question of time and place

The short answer as to when it is best to drink Scotch whisky is any time you feel like it. In practice many outside factors must influence the matter. Extremes of temperature, whether of heat or cold, are one obvious factor. The state of mind and body are another. Clearly a dram is likely to be savoured with more appreciation after a day in the open air rather than in the smoky atmosphere of a city when no exercise has been taken. Scotch whisky can best be savoured in Scotland itself where it was distilled, but it travels well around the world and provides a taste of Scotland anywhere at any time. In the subsequent pages I have indicated that some malt whiskies may perhaps best be savoured before and some after a meal, but this is purely a pointer and not in any sense a firm guide. Everyone should make their own decisions on this score.

Independent bottling

There is nothing to stop anyone buying malt whisky in the cask and storing it to have it bottled for themselves when they wish. In practice it is a very sensible way of buying malt whisky and various societies and syndicates with a special interest in malt whisky do so. Two independent bottlers in particular are also well known for the practice. These are Gordon & MacPhail Ltd, 58-60 South St, Elgin, Morayshire, IV30 1YJ and William Cadenhead Ltd, 172 Canongate, Edinburgh, EH8 8BN. Anyone interested in malt whisky owes a debt to these firms for providing many single malts which would otherwise be unobtainable. The Scotch Malt Whisky Society, situated at The Vaults, Leith, 87 Giles St, Edinburgh, EH6 6BZ, performs a like service for some 16,000 members. On the other hand since these bottlings vary considerably in age and strength it is unfair and unreasonable to attempt to describe a distillery's malt whisky from them. They are like an old, long bottled vintage port, delightful and rewarding, but unrepeatable and not representative of modern standard bottlings.

Publicity regarding distilleries

The Scotch Whisky Heritage Centre, 358 Castlehill, Edinburgh, open seven days a week, (tel: 031 220 0441) by the Castle entrance, is fun and informative for visitors of any age and sex, from family parties to organised groups. Here you may learn painlessly all the facts about distilling and you can ride in half a whisky barrel for an audio-visual journey through the centuries giving all the information on Scotch Whisky anyone could want in six languages. Whisky tastings are also arranged. The Cairngorm Whisky Centre and Museum at Aviemore is also worth visiting, as is the old distillery at Dallas Dhu near Forres. (See p.00). The Scottish Tourist Board at Ravelston Crescent, Edinburgh (tel: 031 332 2433) and local tourist offices in the Grampian and Highland Regions will also give details of those distilleries open for visitors, or on The Whisky Trail. Even where they have reception centres, however, their main task is distilling whisky, so it is advisable to telephone beforehand.

Particulars of distilleries

It is important to know where each distillery is, a little of its background history, so that one can judge how much continuity and experience lies behind it, also who exactly owns it and to whom it is licensed, both very pertinent points. If you happen to be in the area it is as well to know whether you can visit it and whether it is accustomed to dealing with visitors. Finally, some idea of what the product tastes like cannot come amiss. From the particulars of the distilleries that follows in alphabetical order the reader should learn quite a lot about the making of malt whisky and the development of the industry itself.

The individual choice

Since all taste is a matter for the individual to make up his or her own mind about, it is impossible to do more than make suggestions and point the individual in the right direction. The basic information is here. It is up to each reader to go on as far as he wishes in his or her own way. It has often been argued that there is no such thing as bad Scotch whisky and it is up to everyone to make their own choice. There is certainly a great deal of satisfaction to be had from any Scotch whisky distilled in Scotland, but in the ensuing pages we are concerned with the original Scotch whisky which was distilled before the invention of the patent-still. In discovering the infinite variety and satisfaction to be had from the malt whiskies, distilled in the pot-stills of Scotland, the reader who has never sampled them before should find great enjoyment. Even those who have already grown to know and savour the flavours of the various malt whiskies may learn something from what follows. *Slainte!*

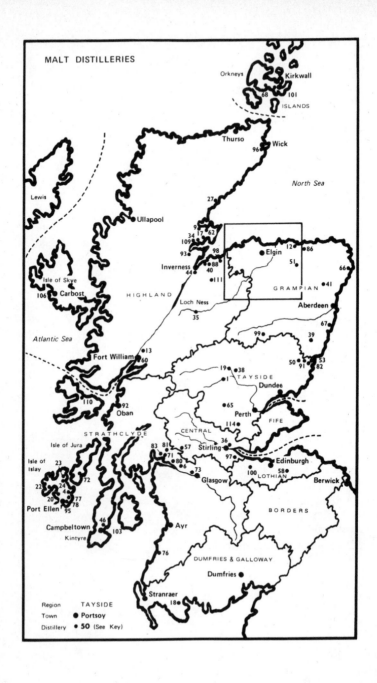

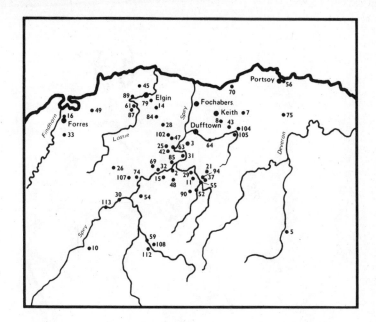

1 Aberfeldy	39 Fettercairn	77 Lagavulin
2 Aberlour	40 Glen Albyn	78 Laphroaig
3 Allt-A-Bhainne	41 Glen Garioch	79 Linkwood
4 Ardbeg	42 Glen Grant	80 Littlemill
5 Ardmore	43 Glen Keith	81 Loch Lomond
6 Auchentoshan	44 Glen Mhor	82 Lochside
7 Auchroisk	45 Glen Moray	83 Lomond
8 Aultmore	46 Glen Scotia	84 Longmorn
9 Balblair	47 Glen Spey	85 Macallan
10 Balmenach	48 Glenallachie	86 Macduff
11 Balvenie	49 Glenburgie	87 Mannochmore
12 Banff	50 Glencadam	88 Millburn
13 Ben Nevis	51 Glendronach	89 Miltonduff
14 Benriach	52 Glendullan	90 Mortlach
15 Benrinnes	53 Glenesk	91 North Port
16 Benromach	54 Glenfarclas	92 Oban
17 Ben Wyvis	55 Glenfiddich	93 Ord
18 Bladnoch	56 Glenlassaugh	94 Pittyvaich
19 Blair Athol	57 Glengoyne	95 Port Ellen
20 Bowmore	58 Glenkinchie	96 Pulteney
21 Braes of Glenlivet	59 The Glenlivet	97 Rosebank
22 Bruichladdich	60 Glenlochy	98 Royal Brackla
23 Bunnahabhain	61 Glenlossie	99 Royal Lochnagar
24 Caol Ila	62 Glenmorangie	100 St Magdalene
25 Caperdonich	63 Glenrothes	101 Scapa
26 Cardhu	64 Glentauchers	102 Speyburn
27 Clynelish	65 Glenturret	103 Springbank
28 Coleburn	66 Glenugie	104 Strathisla
29 Convalmore	67 Glenury Royal	105 Strathmill
30 Cragganmore	68 Highland Park	106 Talisker
31 Craigellachie	69 Imperial	107 Tamdhu
32 Dailuaine	70 Inchgower	108 Tamnavulin-Glenlivet
33 Dallas Dhu	71 Inverleven	109 Teaninich
34 Dalmore	72 Isle of Jura	110 Tobermory
35 Dalwhinnie	73 Kinclaith	111 Tomatin
36 Deanston	74 Knockandoo	112 Tomintoul-Glenlivet
37 Dufftown-Glenlivet	75 Knockdhu	113 Tormore
38 Edradour	76 Ladyburn	114 Tullibardine

44

ABERFELDY

Situation
Aberfeldy, Perthshire. 32 miles north-west of Perth. Tayside Region

Classification
Highland (Southern)

Origins and background
Built by the Dewar brothers, John and Tommy, in the 1890s near where their father had been born. It may possibly have been intended as a memorial to him, but it was more probably seen as a seal on his and their success story, from crofters to distilling magnates in two generations. On their merger with the DCL in 1925 it became a part of the DCL empire, now themselves merged into United Distillers plc.

Owned by
United Distillers

Visitors
Reception Centre. Tel: 0887 20330

Age and strength when bottled
Obtainable only through Gordon & MacPhail Ltd

Comments
Almost all used for blending and presumably most of it goes into John Dewar's blends. It is hard to say more on one tasting than that it seems a clean light-bodied highland malt whisky. This certainly seems to be one which should be more freely available in its own right, like so many others which are seldom obtained except through the independent bottlers.

ABERLOUR

Situation
Near Ben Rinnes south of Dufftown, in the Spey Valley.
Grampian Region

Classification
Highland (Speyside)

Origins and background
A distillery was first built here in 1826 by James Gordon.
Subsequently a second distillery was built on the site in
1879 by a local banker, James Fleming. It was severely
damaged by fire and was sold in 1892 to R. Thorne and
Sons Ltd. They rebuilt and expanded it. It was bought by
S. Campbell & Son Ltd in 1945 but in 1974 they were taken
over by Pernod Ricard, now part of Ricard International
SA. Like so many Speyside distilleries, it is delightfully
positioned close to the Spey and well screened from the
road by a pine wood. Its water comes from the Well
of Drostan, which has connections with St Dunstan
and Glastonbury. The present distillery has been com-
prehensively modernised and as might be expected the
malt whisky it produces has been widely sold in France.

Owned by
Ricard International SA

Visitors
Reception Centre. Tel: 03405 204

Age and strength when bottled
12 years at 43% **volume**

Comments
This is a very good, clean post-prandial dram, full bodied
and smooth with no need to cling on to the Glenlivet affix,
which has led to this being termed the longest Glen in
Scotland.

ALLT-A-BHAINNE (*alt-a-bane*)

Situation
4 miles south west of Dufftown on the slopes of Ben Rinnes. Grampian Region

Classification
Highland (Speyside)

Origins and background
The name Allt-a-Bhainne means in Gaelic the milk burn, signifying in this case perhaps a smooth malt whisky. Opened in 1975 by Seagrams at a cost of £2.7 million this distillery uses the most modern equipment and is very carefully landscaped to fit in with the surrounding countryside. Its capacity of about one million proof gallons, or 2.595 million litres of alcohol, was doubled in 1989. This is one of the latest distilleries to open in the region. Unfortunately as yet none has been bottled as a malt whisky.

Owned by
Seagram Distillers plc

Visitors
By arrangement

Age and strength when bottled
None as yet bottled

Comments
The malt whisky is said to be smooth and clean but is not yet on sale to the public.

ARDBEG

Situation
Port Ellen, Islay, Argyll. Strathclyde Region

Classification
Islay

Origins and background
Established by the McDougall family around 1815 on a site used originally for illicit distilling this distillery remained privately owned until taken over by Hiram Walker in 1979. The water is obtained from two lochs inland from the distillery, Loch Arinambeast and Loch Uigeadale. The local barley and local peat are also used and production is only around 300,000 proof gallons a year, or 778,500 litres of alcohol, mostly used in blending. The distillery was closed, but re-opened in 1989.

Owned by
Allied Distillers Ltd

Visitors
No

Age and strength when bottled
10 years at 40% volume

Comments
This is a distinctively Islay malt whisky, unmistakeably west coast. It has a full body and also a distinctive iodine aftermath. It is definitely an after-dinner drink and it is decidedly good news that the distillery has re-opened.

ARDMORE

Situation
At Kennethmont, 17 miles south of Huntly. Grampian Region

Classification
Highland (Speyside)

Origins and background
Built by William Teacher's sons in 1891 when they realised the importance of having their own direct access to supplies of malt whisky for blending purposes. It was modernised and greatly enlarged in the 1950s, when William Teacher remained one of the largest independent whisky distillers still in the control of the original family. They were taken over by Allied Breweries in 1976 and are now part of Allied Distillers Ltd.

Owned by
Allied Distillers Ltd

Visitors
By arrangement

Age and strength when bottled
18 years at 46% volume

Comments
This has always been retained by William Teacher and Sons as the basis for their famous blend and as such only a little has found its way onto the market through the independent bottlers. From a sample bottled by Wm Cadenhead at 18 years and 46% volume it appears to be a reasonable after-dinner dram with a pleasing aroma and aftermath. It should merit bottling.

AUCHENTOSHAN

Situation
Ten miles north of Glasgow at Duntocher, Dunbartonshire.
Strathclyde Region

Classification
Lowland

Origins and background
Established in 1825 on the road from Glasgow to Dumbarton it was badly damaged by bombs during the 1939-45 War
but was completely rebuilt and modernised. Acquired in
1984 by Stanley P. Morrison Ltd, still a private company,
but now Morrison, Bowmore Distillers Ltd. (See Bowmore
and Glen Garioch.) It lies just below the 'Highland Line'
so the whisky is technically a Lowland malt although peat
and water are obtained from north of the 'Line'. The latter
is from Loch Cochno in the Kilpatrick Hills. The distilling
process is unusual in that three stills are used instead of
the customary two. The whisky is therefore triple-distilled
and possibly this may be responsible for producing a
lighter malt than usual.

Owned by
Morrison Bowmore Distillers Ltd

Visitors
Reception centre. Tel: 038976 561

Age and strength when bottled
It is sold at 5, 8, 10, 12 and 18 years at 40% volume

Comments
Perhaps because of its special triple distillation it is a very
light and clean tasting dram at 5 and 10 years, but best
at 12 or possibly 18 years with more body than might be
expected.

AUCHROISK

Situation
Mulben, Banffshire. Grampian Region

Classification
Highland (Speyside)

Origins and background
Auchroisk is somewhat unusual, being newly built in 1974 by the International Distillers and Vintners Ltd, and taking its name from a nearby farm, the Gaelic meaning of which is 'the forest of the red stream'. The water for the distillery is drawn from a spring known as Dorie's Well and from a tributary of the Spey, the Mulben Burn. As might be expected the buildings are extremely modern but blend well with the countryside. The investment amounted to £1 million and the eight stills have a production capacity of 1.5 million gallons, or 3.8925 million litres of alcohol. The malt whisky is marketed under the name **The Singleton** on the pretext that Auchroisk is not easily pronounced.

Owned by
International Distillers & Vintners Ltd

Visitors
Reception Centre. Tel: 05426 333

Age and strength when bottled
10 years old at 40% volume

Comments
Although a brand new distillery the malt whisky produced is a pleasing, smooth after-dinner dram with a good aftermath. Clearly a lot must go for blending, but it is readily available.

AULTMORE

Situation
About 3 miles from Keith and 9 miles from Buckie. Grampian Region

Classification
Highland (Speyside)

Origins and background
The distillery was originally built in 1896 by Alexander Edward of Sanquhar. In 1899 as Managing Director of a company with the resounding title of The Oban and Aultmore Glenlivet Distillery Co. Ltd, Alexander Edward relinquished ownership to the newly formed Company, which controlled both distilleries. In the hard times of 1923 Aultmore was acquired by John Dewar & Sons Ltd, thus becoming part of the DCL and hence now part of United Distillers plc under overall control of Guinness plc.

Owned by
United Distillers

Visitors
Welcome. Tel: 05442 2397/2762

Age and strength when bottled
12 years old at 40% volume

Comments
At one time apparently regarded as being in 'the longest glen in Scotland' it no longer flaunts the misleading Glenlivet affix and has no need to do so. Although quite a lot must go for blending this malt whisky is readily available and makes a very good after-dinner drink. It is a good smooth dram with a clean dry aftermath.

BALBLAIR

Situation
Edderton, near Tain, Ross-shire. Highland Region

Classification
Highland (Northern)

Origins and background
Dating back to 1790, or possibly even earlier to around 1750, this distillery may claim to be amongst the oldest in Scotland. The distillery on the present site, however, dates from 1872 when it was very greatly developed by Andrew Ross & Son, the owners at that time. Edderton is well supplied with both ample peat and water, which is of course a considerable asset to the distillery. It was acquired by Hiram Walker in 1969. It is considered a fast maturing malt whisky.

Owned by
Allied Distillers Ltd

Visitors
Reception Centre. Tel: 066262 273

Age and strength when bottled
5 years at 40% volume

Comments
Most of this malt whisky goes for blending, but some is bottled, mainly for export, and some is bottled by the independent bottlers Gordon & MacPhail. At 5 years, possibly a trifle young, but a pleasing light and rather dry dram with clean aftermath, which is much appreciated by the Italians.

BALMENACH

Situation
Balmenach, Cromdale, Grantown-on-Spey, Morayshire.
Grampian Region

Classification
Highland (Speyside)

Origins & Background
The original founder was one James MacGregor, who was
undoubtedly an illicit distiller when he started in 1801, but
he took out a license in 1824 and the distillery officially
dates from then. As well as founding the distillery and
running it for many years James MacGregor was the
grandfather of Robert Bruce Lockhart who describes it
delightfully in his book, *Scotch*. In the same great storm
of 28th December 1879 which caused the Tay Bridge disaster the distillery chimney stack collapsed and there was
nearly a fire, but the situation was saved by the stillman
who opened the discharge cocks and allowed the spirit
to run out thus preventing the fire spreading. In 1897 the
grandson of the founder formed the Balmenach-Glenlivet
Distillery Ltd, thus adding the affix Glenlivet to the product. In 1922 during the lean post-war years control passed
to DCL, hence to United Distillers plc.

Owned by
United Distillers

Visitors
Reception Centre. Tel: 0479 2569

Age and strength when bottled
24 years at 46% volume by William Cadenhead Ltd

Comments
Unfortunately today it is only available through the independent bottlers and it is unfair to compare a 24 year
old with 8 and 12 year old drams. This was certainly an
interesting after-dinner dram indicating that it would be
worth bottling it.

BALVENIE

Situation
Dufftown, Banffshire. Grampian Region

Classification
Highland (Speyside)

Origins and background
Dufftown is now rated as Scotland's whisky capital since
the eclipse of Campbeltown. A local jingle runs:
　　'Rome was built on seven hills
　　Dufftown stands on seven stills.'
The distillery was established in 1890 by William Grant on
part of the land he had bought for his nearby Glenfiddich
distillery. The water for distilling is obtained from the fine
Robbie Dubh spring and both distilleries use the nearby
Fiddich Burn for cooling purposes. Still owned by the
firm of William Grant & Sons Ltd, the distillery was greatly
expanded in 1955. Balvenie now has its own maltings and
supplies malt for Glenfiddich which has its own bottling
plant and in return bottles for Balvenie.

Owned by
William Grant & Sons Ltd

Visitors
Welcome at neighbouring Glenfiddich visitors centre

Age and strength when bottled
No age given at 40% and 43% volume

Comments
The Balvenie Founders reserve at 40% volume is a vatting
of distillates from casks of between 10 and 12 years. It has
an initially sweet approach and very satisfying aftermath.
The Balvenie Classic at 43% volume is vatted from casks
at least 12 years old and is not surprisingly a little richer
and more mellow with an even longer aftermath. Both
are very good drams, but with no resemblance to nearby
Glenfiddich.

BEN NEVIS

Situation
Ben Nevis, Fort William, Inverness-shire. Highland Region

Classification
Highland (Western)

Origins and background
Built in 1825 by 'Long John' Macdonald, a local farmer turned distiller, who claimed descent from the Lords of the Isles and was noted for his outstanding physique as well as the fact that he stood the then remarkable height of 6 feet 4 inches. He presented Queen Victoria with a cask of Ben Nevis malt whisky on her visit to Fort William in 1848 and on his death in 1856 was succeeded by his son Donald, who in turn was succeeded by his son John. The Ben Nevis Distillers (Fort William) Ltd, was formed to run the distillery and in 1981 it was acquired by Long John International Limited, a subsidiary of Seager Evans and Whitbread & Co. Ltd. It was sold to Allied Lyons who in turn sold it to the Nikka Company of Japan. It has been closed for some years but distilling is due to start again in 1990.

Owned by
Nikka Distillers

Visitors
By arrangement

Age and strength when bottled
Independently bottled at 19 years and 46% volume

Comments
Bottled by William Cadenhead at 19 years and 46% volume. It is impossible to say much more than that if this is typical it is not surprising that most of it is used in blending.

BENRIACH

Situation
Next to Longmorn just south of Elgin, Morayshire.
Grampian Region

Classification
Highland

Origins and background
Built by John Duff in the whisky boom of the 1890s next to
the Longmorn distillery. It has plentiful supplies of local
spring water and peat from Mannoch Hill. It was closed
from 1903 to 1965, but has been producing a very good
whisky since then, although only bottled by the independent bottlers.

Owned by
The Seagram Company Ltd

Visitors
By arrangement. Tel: 05422 7471

Age and strength when bottled
13 years and 46% volume

Comments
Although close to Longmorn, nothing like as exceptional,
but still light and extremely delicate. Apparently almost
all that is distilled goes for blending. It is surprising that
some is not bottled by the distillers rather than only by the
independent bottlers Gordon and MacPhail.

BENRINNES

Situation
Benrinnes, Aberlour, Banffshire. Grampian Region

Classification
Highland (Speyside)

Origins and background
Naturally the distillery is named after nearby Ben Rinness from which it obtains its water supplies. It was built in 1897 towards the very end of the Scotch whisky boom and operated successfully and independently until the lean years after the First World War. It was then acquired by John Dewar & Sons Ltd who took it over under their name in 1926. With their takeover by DCL it was transferred to the Scottish Malt Distillers Ltd, and passed to the present License holders. It has continued operating since then except for very brief closures at the start of the 1930s and in 1943 during the last War.

Owned by
United Distillers

Visitors
Reception Centre. Tel: 03405 215

Age and strength when bottled
Bottled independently at 18 years and 46% Proof

Comments
It is unfortunate that this is only obtainable through the independent bottlers but it is regarded highly by them and makes a very pleasing aperitif with a delicate dry peaty aftermath.

BEN WYVIS

Situation
Invergordon. Highland Region

Classification
Highland (Northern)

Origins and background
Sited below Ben Wyvis (3,429 ft) from which it gets its name, the distillery is actually within the Invergordon distillery complex, next to the most northern patent still grain distillery. It was built in 1965 and so far has only been used for blending with none bottled as a malt whisky. Owned by The Invergordon Distillers Ltd.

Visitors
By arrangement

Age and strength when bottled
None bottled

Comments
The assumption must be that it is not considered good enough, but it is a pity the general public are not given the chance to decide that for themselves.

BLADNOCH

Situation
1 mile south-east of Wigtown. Dumfries & Galloway
Region

Classification
Lowland (South West)

Origins
This most southerly of all the Scottish malt distilleries was
founded in 1817 by the McClelland family at the lower end
of the village of Bladnoch from which it takes its name.
It has had a somewhat varied history with three distinct
periods of expansion followed by temporary closures.
After changing hands a number of times it was finally
closed for 18 years from the start of the 1939-45 War years,
during which period it even had the stills removed and
sent to Sweden. It was only re-opened in 1956, changing
hands several more times until bought by Arthur Bell &
Sons in 1983 from Inver House Distillers Ltd, hence now
controlled by United Distillers plc.

Owned by
United Distillers

Visitors
Reception Centre. Tel: 09884 2235

Age and strength when bottled
8 years at 40% volume

Comments
This lowland malt whisky is a very pleasing smooth dram
with a light clean flavour and surprising aftermath.

BLAIR ATHOL

Situation
Blair Athol, Pitlochry, Perthshire. Tayside Region

Classification
Highland (Central)

Origins and background
Said to have been founded in 1825 this distillery obtains its water from the Kinnaird Burn and the mountain springs of Ben Vrackie above Pitlochry. Although misleadingly named after the village close to the ducal seat at Blair Castle it has an attractive position in this well-known tourist centre. It was initially run by Alexander Connacher & Co., but was acquired by P. Mackenzie & Co., Distillers Ltd, of Edinburgh, who greatly enlarged it. After the lean 1914-18 War years it was closed until bought by Arthur Bell & Sons Ltd, in 1949 when it was rebuilt. In 1973 the number of stills was doubled from two to four. Since 1988 it has been controlled by United Distillers plc.

Owned by
United Distillers

Visitors
Reception Centre. Tel: 0796 2234

Age and strength when bottled
8 years at 40% volume

Comments
A lot of this is no doubt used for blending by Arthur Bell & Sons, but it is readily available as a malt whisky. It is an interesting full-bodied dry dram with very little aftermath which makes a good drink before a meal.

BOWMORE

Situation
Isle of Islay, on the shore of Loch Indaal and actually right on the sea.

Classification
West Coast Islay

Origins and background
Bowmore was founded in 1779 by a Mr Simson and is the second oldest distillery on Islay. It was expanded by a James Mutter in the late 19th century until the 1890s when it was taken over by the Bowmore Distillery Co. Ltd. It has now been acquired by the Morrison Bowmore Distillers Ltd.

Owned by
Morrison Bowmore Distillers Ltd.

Visitors
Reception centre. Tel: 049681 441

Age and strength when bottled
12 years and 40% volume

Comments
A smooth and pleasing after-dinner Islay malt whisky, without quite as much of the heaviness characteristic of many of the Islay malts and with a distinct character of its own.

BRACKLA: *see* ROYAL BRACKLA

BRAES OF GLENLIVET

Situation
9 miles south west of Dufftown, The Braes of Glenlivet.
Grampian Region

Classification
Highland (Speyside)

Origins and background
Opened in 1973 by Seagram Distillers plc, when they still
had not taken over The Glenlivet Distillers. Hence the reason at the time of building this distillery for the addition
of the Glenlivet affix to the name, although it does in fact
have more reason for the addition than many others, being
closer to the Glenlivet distillery than any other. Although
the design of the distillery is fairly traditional it naturally
employs all the latest engineering and production tech-
niques. It has a capacity of over a million proof gallons
a year or 2.595 million litres of alcohol. Two wells close
to the distillery, the Preenie and Kate's Well, provide the
water supply for the distilling process.

Owned by
Seagram Distillers plc

Visitors
By arrangement

Age and strength when bottled
All is used for blending

Comments
This should be a very interesting malt whisky if any was
freed for consumption by the public.

BRORA: *see* CLYNELISH

BRUICHLADDICH *(brewichladdie)*

Situation
Bruichladdich, Isle of Islay, Argyll. Strathclyde Region

Classification
Islay

Origins and background
This is another Islay distillery right on the sea. It was
built in 1881 by the Harvey family, well known distillers,
who formed John and Robert Harvey Limited. From 1886
onwards they ran their Islay distillery as the Bruichladdich
Distillery Co. (Islay) Ltd, and it continued thus until its
closure in 1938 and acquisition ultimately by the National
Distillers of America, who controlled it through a holding
company Train & McIntyre, who incorporated it into
their distilling side, Associated Scottish Distillers. After
further changes of ownership the distillery was acquired
by Invergordon Distillers Ltd in 1968 and remains with
them today, with the addition of two new stills and general
expansion so that it now has a capacity of 800,000 proof
gallons or 2,076,000 litres of alcohol. Its water supplies are
obtained from an inland reservoir.

Owned by
Invergordon Distillers Ltd

Visitors
Reception Centre. Tel: 049685 221

Age and strength when bottled
10 years at 40% volume

Comments
Perhaps because its water supply comes from inland this
is not like many other Islay malt whiskies. It is a very good
aperitif, light and peaty and although a very pleasing dram
it is not as heavy as others on Islay.

BUNNAHABHAIN *(bunahavan)*

Situation
Bunnahabhain, Port Askaig, Islay, Argyll. Strathclyde Region

Classification
Islay

Origins and background
Built on the north-east coast of Islay, Bunnahabhain started distilling in 1883. The Islay Distillery Co., which controlled the distillery, merged in 1887 to become part of the Highland Distilleries Company plc, which controls the notable blend The Famous Grouse taken over in 1970 along with Matthew Gloag & Son Ltd. Since that date the group has expanded remarkably. Until recently almost all the product of the distillery was utilised for blending.

Owned by
The Highland Distilleries Co. plc

Visitors
Reception Centre. Tel: 049684 646

Age and strength when bottled
12 years at 40% volume

Comments
A good after-dinner dram, but not obviously an Islay malt whisky, although with a full bodied flavour it leaves a good aftermath.

CAOL ILA *(coal eela)*

Situation
Caol Ila, Port Askaig, Islay, Argyll. Strathclyde Region

Classification
Islay

Origins and background
Possibly founded around 1846 Caol Ila is situated in the most sheltered bay on Islay north of Port Askaig and overlooking the Sound of Jura. It has its own private wharf through which it obtains its own barley and ships off its whisky in return. It gets its water supplies from Loch Torrabus, said to be the finest on Islay. The owners from 1880 to 1920 were Bulloch Lade & Co. Ltd, who were a subsidiary of Robertson & Baxter Ltd. In 1920 they formed Caol Ila Distillery Co. Ltd, to run the distillery. When DCL took them over in 1927 the management reverted to Bulloch Lade & Co. Ltd. Only a limited amount is available on the home market, apart from the independent bottlers, but it is available overseas under the name Glen Isla.

Owned by
United Distillers

Visitors
Reception Centre. Tel: 049684 207

Age and strength when bottled
12 years old at 40% volume

Comments
A very light coloured pleasing pre-prandial dram, not as round bodied as many on Islay, but with an attractive aftermath.

CAPERDONICH

Situation
Rothes, Morayshire. Grampian Region

Classification
Highland (Speyside)

Origins and background
In 1897 Major James Grant, son of Elgin lawyer, James
Grant, founder of the Glen Grant distillery at Rothes,
decided to build a second distillery across the road from
the first named Glen Grant 2, joining the two distilleries
by a pipe, which mixed the two malts produced. Following the crash of the 1890s the No. 2 distillery was
closed down in 1901. It was rebuilt in 1965 and renamed
the Caperdonich Distillery Ltd, using the name of the
Caperdonich Well from which the water was obtained
for the original Glen Grant distillery, and which has never
been known to run dry.

Owned by
The Seagram Co. Ltd

Visitors
Welcome. Tel: 05422 7471

Age and strength when bottled
Only available from the independent bottlers so varies

Comments
Similar, hardly surprisingly, to its neighbour Glen Grant,
if perhaps not in quite the same class, although since it is
rarely available it is hard to say. It seems to be a pleasing
after-dinner dram with a good aftermath. It is a shame that
it is not more readily available.

CARDHU *(cardoo)*

Situation
Knockando, Morayshire. Grampian Region

Classification
Highland (Speyside)

Origins and background
Founded in 1824 by John Cummings on a site where
whisky had been distilled for many years illicitly. A
second distillery close by was built in 1855, when the
first had fallen into disrepair. It was bought by John
Walker & Sons Ltd in 1893 and greatly expanded. Its
water supply is piped from Mannoch Hill two miles to
the northwest and the distillery also gets its peat from
the same site. It was extensively modernised in 1965 and
the whisky is known as Cardhu. The distillery was often
known as Cardow which is merely a different spelling of
the nearby hamlet sited on the banks of the Spey.

Owned by
United Distillers

Visitors
Reception Centre. Tel: 03406 204

Age and strength when bottled
12 years at 40% volume

Comments
Smooth and clean with a good slightly sweet aftermath
this is a very sound after-dinner Speyside malt whisky.

CLYNELISH *(clyne-leesh)*

Situation
Brora, Sutherland. Highland Region

Classification
Highland (Northern)

Licensees
Ainslie & Heilbron (Distillers) Ltd

Origins and background
Originally built in 1819 by the Duke of Sutherland, then Marquis of Stafford, to provide a market for the grain of the crofters forcibly moved to the coast as a result of the Clearances. It was originally called the Brora distillery and was sited next to the Brora coalfield to provide ready power, but the coal proved second-rate for the purpose, although the whisky distilled was highly regarded. Subsequently in 1896 James Ainslie and Co. took over the distillery and completely rebuilt it about a mile further away on the east coast. Despite the collapse of the whisky boom at the turn of the century James Ainslie & Co. continued in business until 1912 when the DCL acquired a considerable shareholding. The Clynelish Distillery Co. Ltd was then formed and the distillery renamed. In 1925 DCL took over completely and built a new malt whisky distillery beside Clynelish, which was given the old name Brora, but it has since been dismantled and closed. It may now become a visitor centre.

Owned by
United Distillers

Visitors
Reception Centre. Tel: 0408 21444

Age and strength when bottled
12 years at 40% volume

Comments
A rather peaty and very interesting after-dinner dram with an extremely good aftermath.

COLEBURN

Situation
Longmorn, by Elgin, Morayshire. Grampian Region

Classification
Highland (Speyside)

Origins and background
The distillery was built in 1896 by John Robertson & Son Ltd, trying like many others to cash in on the seemingly ever upwards spiral of the Scotch whisky boom of the nineties. During the early years of the present century the distillery was the subject for several successful experiments in the purification of industrial effluents. The process developed at Coleburn was utilised in a number of distilleries elsewhere in the area. The distillery was taken over in 1916 by the Clynelish Distillery Co. Ltd, and in 1930 it was acquired by the Scottish Malt Distillers Ltd, a subsidiary of the DCL. The malt produced was mostly used for distilling but some was bottled independently by Wm Cadenhead Ltd. It has been closed for some years.

Owned by
United Distillers

Visitors
Only by arrangement

Age and strength when bottled
Only available through the independent bottlers

Comments
In view of the proximity of such a rare malt whisky as Longmorn it is a pity this is not bottled by the distillery. Judging by the independent bottlings it seems an interesting light and clean tasting dram, but not up to its neighbour's standards.

CONVALMORE

Situation
Dufftown, Banffshire. Grampian Region

Classification
Highland (Speyside)

Origins and background
Another of the Dufftown distilleries, it draws its water from the nearby Conval hills from which it also obtains its name. It was built originally in 1894 by the Convalmore-Glenlivet Distillery Co. Ltd, but was acquired by W. P. Lowrie & Co. Ltd, in 1904, who was in turn taken over by James Buchanan & Co. Ltd, in 1906. It was then severely damaged by fire in 1909 and extensively damaged. In the re-building process a continuous wash still was included, a considerable innovation at the time, but this experimental plant proved faulty and was abandoned in 1915, when they reverted to the old pot-still methods. In 1925 with the merger of Buchanan-Dewar with DCL the distillery effectively came under the DCL control. It has now been closed for some years.

Owned by
United Distillers

Visitors
By arrangement

Age and strength when bottled
Varies with the independent bottlers

Comments
Only bottled independently and on the evidence available seems a sound enough full-bodied after-dinner dram. On the face of it, it should be worth bottling by the distillers, but at present it almost all goes for blending.

CRAGGANMORE

Situation
Ballindalloch, Banffshire. Grampian Region

Classification
Highland (Speyside)

Origins and background
Built in 1869 by John Smith, who had left his employer at
The Glenlivet Distillery to branch out as a self-employed
farmer and distiller on his own account. A man of considerable strength and magnificent physique he is reputed
to have moved a large stone which stands at the entrance
to the distillery by his own efforts when it obstructed his
plough. In the course of so doing he uncovered a hidden
treasure and flourished exceedingly thereafter. His son
Gordon Smith inherited the distillery from his father and
on his death in 1923 it was sold to a syndicate who formed
the Cragganmore Distillery Co. Ltd. A leading member of
the syndicate was Peter J. Mackie, later Sir Peter Mackie,
of White Horse Distillers Ltd. In 1965 the remaining shareholders were bought out and the distillery was taken over
by the DCL, hence is now part of United Distillers plc.

Owned by
United Distillers

Visitors
By appointment. Tel: 08072 202

Age and strength when bottled
12 years at 40% volume

Comments
Recently more readily available, but the bulk still goes
for blending. It seems to be well worth bottling. It is
a good, dry and delicate interesting after-dinner dram,
possibly more west coast in character rather than typically Speyside.

CRAIGELLACHIE

Situation
Craigellachie, Banffshire. Grampian Region

Classification
Highland (Speyside)

Origins and background
Built in 1890 by Peter J. Mackie in partnership with Alexander Edward, as the Craigellachie-Glenlivet Distillery Ltd, but eventually taken over completely by Peter Mackie. It stands impressively above the well known single-span Craigellachie bridge across the River Spey and the Craigellachie Rock. When Mackie & Co., Distillers, Ltd, were taken over in 1924 by the DCL to be transformed into White Horse Distillers Limited, the distillery became part of the DCL empire.

Owned by
United Distillers

Visitors
Reception Centre. Tel: 03404 212/228

Age and strength when bottled
It is all used for blending and is only available through the independent bottlers.

Comments
This is another malt whisky which should on the evidence available be bottled at least in small quantities. It seems a light and clean after-dinner dram.

DAILUAINE

Situation
Carron, Morayshire. Grampian Region

Classification
Highland (Speyside)

Origins and background
The distillery was built in the shadow of Ben Rinnes in 1852, but was completely renovated and rebuilt at the start of the whisky boom in the early 1890s by Thomas Mackenzie. A merger between Daluaine-Glenlivet Distillers Ltd, and Talisker Distillery Ltd, in 1898 led to the formation of the Daluaine-Talisker Distilleries Ltd. They were acquired in 1916 jointly by Dewar, DCL, W. P. Lowrie and Johnnie Walker, before all came under the DCL umbrella in 1925.

Owned by
United Distillers

Visitors
Reception Centre. Tel: 03406 361/362

Age and strength when bottled
Only bottled by the independent bottlers

Comments
On the evidence of an 18 year old at 46% a very reasonable Speyside after-dinner dram and yet another which on this showing should merit at least a limited amount of bottling by the distiller instead of allowing it all to go for blending.

DALMORE

Situation
Alness, Ross-shire. Highland Region

Classification
Highland (Northern)

Origins and background
Splendidly placed overlooking the Black Isle and the Cromarty Firth, with the sole rights to take water from the river Alness, the Dalmore distillery was founded in 1839 and was taken over by Mackenzie Brothers in 1867, still the present owners. Although they merged with Whyte & Mackay Ltd in 1960 they had a Mackenzie of the third generation serving on the board until 1988. Although one of the stills in use dates back to 1874 the distillery has a record of adopting modern methods of production and its capacity is 1.2 million gallons, or 3.114 million litres of alcohol. During the World War the distillery was taken over by the Royal Navy for the assembling of mines and because of this did not start distilling again until 1922. The bulk of the malt goes to make up Whyte & Mackay's blends, but some is bottled.

Owned by
Whyte & Mackay Distillers Ltd

Visitors
Reception Centre. Tel: 0349882 362

Age and strength when bottled
12 years at 40% volume

Comments
A rather dry but very pleasing heavy after-dinner dram with an interesting aftermath.

DALWHINNIE

Situation
Dalwhinnie, Inverness-shire. Highland Region

Classification
Highland (Central)

Origins and background
Sited in the Pass of Drumochter, the distillery was built in 1898 by Alex Mackenzie and George Sellar of Kingussie at a height of 1,174 feet and it was then claimed to be the highest distillery in Scotland. The Gaelic meaning of Dalwhinnie is 'the meeting place' and it is certainly an area which has lived up to its name over the centuries. Historically it has seen clan battles and Prince Charles' army encamped after the raising of the standard at Glenfinnan in 1745 as he marched down General Wade's military road, which runs through the distillery grounds. The distillery was taken over from the founders by A. P. Blyth & Son who sold it in 1905 to James Munro & Son Ltd, an American syndicate. In 1921 it was sold to Sir James Calder and in 1926 was taken over by J & G Stewart Ltd, but in 1930 went to the Scottish Malt Distillers Ltd, under DCL control. Mostly used for blending but recently promoted successfully as a malt whisky.

Owned by
United Distillers

Visitors
Reception Centre. Tel: 05282 264

Age and strength when bottled
15 years at 43% volume

Comments
Now more widely available, this is a fresh but very smooth malt whisky with a good clean aftermath. A pleasant pre-prandial dram.

DEANSTON

Situation
Doune, Perthshire. Tayside Region

Classification
Highland (Southern)

Origins & background
Built on the site of an old cotton mill on the banks of the river Teith and named after the nearby village of Deanston, it is about a mile from the picturesque Castle Doune. Although it is near to the river, which is good for salmon, the water for the distilling process comes from the Trossachs. The cotton mill dates back to 1785, but when James Finlay & Co. Ltd, the mill-owners, moved elsewhere in 1965 Mr Brodie Hepburn, well known in the whisky industry, saw the potential. Here were large premises well placed on the river Teith, with a water turbine and stand-by generator in working order. He suggested the idea of converting them into a distillery to James Finlay & Co. A deal was agreed whereby James Finlay took two thirds of the equity and Brodie Hepburn Ltd the remainder and overall control. Two wash and two spirit stills were installed and in 1969 production started. Then in 1972 Deanston Distillers Ltd were taken over by Invergordon Distillers Ltd. The distillery has a capacity of 750,000 proof gallons a year, or 1,946,250 litres of alcohol, but was temporarily closed during the mid-1980s recession years.

Owned by
Invergordon Distillers Ltd

Visitors
By arrangement

Age and strength when bottled
Age not given at 40% volume

Comments
A light pre-dinner dram clean, fresh and a touch sweet.

DUFFTOWN-GLENLIVET

Situation
Dufftown, Banffshire. Grampian Region

Classification
Highland (Speyside)

Origins and background
Built in 1896 by P. Mackenzie & Co., Distillers, Ltd, just
to the south of Dufftown in the Dullan Glen this is another
distillery using the hyphenated Glenlivet affix. Despite the
fact that the Dullan and Fiddich burns both flow down
the Dullan Glen to the Spey, it obtains its water supplies
from 'Jock's Well' regarded as ideal for distilling purposes
and noted for its never-failing supply of fine water. In 1933
the distillery was acquired by Arthur Bell & Sons Ltd, at
the start of their steady expansion and this was to become
one of the principal sources of their popular blend. Now
a subsidiary of United Distillers plc.

Owned by
United Distillers

Visitors
Welcome. Tel: 0340 20224/20773

Age and strength when bottled
8 and 10 years at 40% volume

Comments
A light but smooth, very typical Speyside malt whisky and
a good aperitif. The 8 year old, hardly surprisingly, is not
quite up to the standard of the 10 year old. They may feel
they need the Glenlivet affix, but both are sound enough
on their own merits.

EDRADOUR

Situation
Pitlochry, Perthshire. Tayside Region

Classification
Highland (Southern)

Origins and background
Believed to have been founded around 1825 by a group of local farmers the present distillery was probably built around 1837. It was owned by John McIntosh & Co. for many years until finally sold to William Whiteley & Co. Ltd in 1933. In 1938 this company was acquired by a Mr Irving Haim, an American, and remained in his hands for forty years. In 1978 control passed to Mr Delbert Coleman, an American financier, whose holding company was J. G. Turney Ltd. The distillery was then purchased by Pernod Ricard through their subsidiary S. Campbell & Son Ltd, and they are the current owners. It lies beside a burn with steep banks on land leased from the Duke of Atholl. It is widely regarded as the prettiest distillery in Scotland and is certainly the smallest. The spirit still holds under 500 gallons and production rarely exceeds 1,000 gallons a week. More than almost any other distillery it resembles the way a highland distillery was worked in the 19th century. It only employs four men, but they manage the entire operation efficiently and smoothly making this distillery a pleasure to visit. Messrs Pernod Ricard are to be congratulated on not having made any alterations to this showpiece distillery.

Owned by
Ricard International SA

Visitors
Reception Centre. Tel: 0796 2095

Age and strength when bottled
10 years at 40%

Comments
A good clean smooth and light malt whisky with a pleasing aftermath, also bottled by the independent bottlers.

FETTERCAIRN

Situation
Fettercairn, Kincardineshire. Grampian Region

Classification
Highland (East)

Origins and background
The exact date of origin is uncertain but the present distillery was known to be functioning in 1824 and continued distilling under various owners until it was taken over by a local landowner Sir John Gladstone, father of the Prime Minister. Sir John formed the Fettercairn Distillery Co. in 1887. It underwent a long period of closure from the First World War onward until it was bought by the Associated Scottish Distillers Ltd in 1939 for Train & McIntyre. It then passed to Mr Tom Scott Sutherland, an Aberdonian business man, who retained it until 1971 when it was purchased jointly by Hay and MacLeod & Co. and W. & S. Strong & Co. It is now an up-to-date modern distillery with water in plenty from the nearby Grampian Mountains and situated in the fertile Howe o' the Mearns it has plentiful barley supplies at hand. The capacity is about 500,000 proof gallons. The malt whisky produced is known as **Old Fettercairn**. The bulk goes for blending, but some is bottled.

Owned by
Whyte & Mackay Distillers Ltd

Visitors
Reception Centre. Tel: 05614 244

Age and strength when bottled
10 years at 40% volume

Comments
A good clean, dry and satisfying malt whisky which makes pleasing dram before dinner.

GLEN DEVERON: *see* MACDUFF

GLEN ELGIN

Situation
Longmorn, Elgin, Morayshire: Grampian Region

Classification
Highland (Speyside)

Origins and background
It cannot be often that bankers get together to found a
distillery and it is entirely suitable that this should happen
on Speyside where banking, salmon and whisky might all
be considered local industries. In 1900 Mr James Carle and
Mr W. Simpson, both bankers in Elgin, founded this distillery at Longmorn near Glen Rothes in as pleasant a position
as any in the Highlands. It obtains its water supplies from
springs in Glen Rothes. The Glen Elgin-Glenlivet Distillery
Co. Ltd, another hyphenated Glenlivet distillery company,
was formed to run the venture. Then in 1907 J. J. Blanche of
Glasgow took over the company, but in 1936 it was finally
acquired by the Scottish Malt Distillers.

Owned by
United Distillers

Visitors
By arrangement. Tel: 03438 6212

Age and strength when bottled
12 years at 43% volume

Comments
The bulk is used for blending, but as noted some is regu-
larly bottled and sold. It is a typical clean Speyside dram
with a light but pleasing aftermath. This is a good malt
whisky which may be drunk at any time with enjoyment.

GLEN GARIOCH *(glen geery)*

Situation
Old Meldrum, Aberdeenshire. Grampian Region

Classification
Highland (East)

Origins and background
The distillery was reputedly founded in the 1790s and is situated in the village of Old Meldrum not far from Meldrum House, only about twenty miles north west of Aberdeen. It was bought by J F Thomson & Co. of Leith in 1840 and in the 1860s was acquired by William Sanderson & Son, Ltd., blenders of the famous 'Vat 69'. Through them it finally became a part of the DCL empire when they were taken over in 1937, but because of continual water shortages it was never considered very satisfactory, with a capacity of only 140,000 gallons when working normally and eventually in 1968 it was closed. Then in 1970 it was sold to Stanley P. Morrison Ltd of Glasgow who sank a deep well in a nearby field and thus tapped an entirely new source of water. It obtains peat from Pitsligo Moss some ten miles away and with the addition of a new wash still in 1973 has been distilling 500,000 proof gallons annually, or 1,297,500 litres of alcohol, making this a considerable success story. An enterprising side-line is the utilisation of the waste heat from the distillery to heat glasshouses in the grounds for growing fruits and vegetables.

Owned by
Morrison Bowmore Distillers Co. Ltd

Visitors
Reception Centre. Tel: 06512 2706

Age and strength when bottled
10 years at 43% volume and 21 years at 43% volume

Comments
Well marketed, the 10 year old is a very good sound dram which can be recommended at any time. The 21 year old is a smooth full-bodied peaty malt whisky with a fine aftermath.

GLEN GRANT

Situation
Rothes, Morayshire. Grampian Region

Classification
Highland (Speyside)

Origins and background
There has to be something special about the professional
men of Elgin and for that matter the name Grant as well
for it was an Elgin lawyer, James Grant, who in partnership
with his younger brother John in 1840 founded the Glen
Grant distillery on the banks of the Glen Grant burn near
the village of Rothes. They had admittedly been distilling
at nearby Dandaleith since 1834, so they knew what they
were about and it was not long before they were enlarging
their new distillery and producing 40,000 gallons a year.
The introduction of the railway line, which the Grant
family did much to encourage, was a great step forward
from transport by horse to the coast and allowed them
to expand considerably. The distillery was already a very
successful concern when Major James Grant took over
control on his father's death in 1872. It was he who
decided to expand by building another distillery in 1897
across the road from the original one and joined by a
pipe. Called initially Glen Grant No. 2 this was eventually
re-named Caperdonich. (See above) The company, by this
time known as J. & J. Grant, Glen Grant Ltd, merged in
1932 with George and J. G. Smith Ltd to form The Glenlivet
and Glen Grant Distilleries Ltd. In 1970 they merged
with Hill Thomson & Co. Ltd and Longmorn-Glenlivet
Distilleries Ltd, the name of the merged company being
rationalised to The Glenlivet Distillers Ltd. Finally in 1978
they were in turn taken over by Seagram Distillers plc.

Owned by
Seagram Co. Ltd

Visitors
Reception Centre and Museum – On the Whisky Trail. Tel:
03403 413

Age and strength when bottled
No age given at 40% volume, 5 years old at 40% volume and 10 years at 43% volume

Comments
This excellent malt whisky used to be bottled and readily available at 5, 10 and 15 years. Unfortunately it has become too popular selling over 500,000 cases of 5 year old annually in Italy alone. Stock availability has dictated that it is now quite hard to find at any age. It is however a favourite amongst the independent bottlers so all is not lost. The first noted above with no age given is a good dry dram. The second at 5 years old is a pale coloured light and tasty dram which one can understand being popular in Italy and anywhere else. The 10 year old is a medium light very dry and satisfactory malt whisky. Some of the independent bottlings are excellent.

GLEN KEITH

Situation
Keith, Banffshire. Grampian Region

Classification
Highland (Speyside)

Origins and background
In 1957 Seagram Distillers plc bought a flour mill from the
Angus Milling Co. Ltd facing their Strathisla Distillery on
the other bank of the River Isla. After a year's intensive
programme of re-building a new distillery was opened on
the site in 1958. This was the first distillery in Scotland
to use gas-fired stills in place of the traditional coal-fired
stills. The water for distilling is obtained from the Newmill
Spring and peat comes from Knockando. It may be that
the result is not entirely satisfactory as a malt whisky,
but most of the production is used for blending and
none has so far been bottled by the distillery although
a little has been bottled independently. Originally called
the Glenkeith-Glenlivet distillery on the acquisition of The
Glenlivet Distillers the affix was dropped by Seagram.

Owned by
The Seagram Co. Ltd

Visitors
By arrangement. Tel: 05422 7471

Age and strength when bottled
None bottled

Comments
Only available through Gordon & MacPhail it is hard to
say on one sample whether this would be worth bottling
on its own account, but as noted most of the product is
used for blending.

GLEN MORAY

Situation
Elgin, Morayshire. Grampian Region

Classification
Highland (Speyside)

Origins and background
The site of this distillery, founded in 1897 towards the end of the whisky boom, was originally that of the town's West Brewery owned by Henry Arnot & Co. Unfortunately very little appears to have been recorded of its early history until 1920 when it was acquired by Macdonald & Muir Ltd, by which time it had already been closed for a lengthy period. In 1958 the entire distillery underwent a considerable amount of development and enlargement and it now has a capacity of 700,000 gallons a year, or 1,764,000 litres of alcohol. It has also now dropped the Glenlivet affix on its bottlings. Although a great deal is used for blending some is kept aside for bottling at 12 years.

Owned by
Macdonald Martin Distilleries plc

Visitors
Reception centre. Tel: 03432 577

Age and strength when bottled
12 years at 40% volume

Comments
This 12 year old makes a very good, clean mellow all-round dram. It is a good sound example of a light dry Speyside malt whisky.

GLEN SCOTIA

Situation
Campbeltown. Strathclyde Region

Classification
Campbeltown (West Coast)

Origins and background
The distillery was built by the Galbraith family in 1832, close to the Parliament Square in the centre of Campbeltown and was at first named the Scotia. With ample water, peat, coal and barley available locally during the 19th century it was one of the thirty-four distilleries which provided the small town with the proud boast that it was 'the whisky capital of Scotland'. Indifferent distilling and the sale of immature whiskies gave the area a bad name with disastrous results. The Glen Scotia distillery is now one of the only two left. It was owned by A. Gillies & Co. Ltd, but has now been acquired by Barton International plc, who also own Littlemill where it is planned to mature most of of the production from Glen Scotia.

Owned by
Barton International plc

Visitors
By arrangement. Tel: 03897 4154 (Littlemill)

Age and strength when bottled
8 years old at 40% volume

Comments
The malt whisky produced by Glen Scotia has a rich peaty slightly oily taste with an affinity to Irish whiskey, but with a strong and interesting aftermath, making a good dram at any time.

GLEN SPEY

Situation
Rothes, Morayshire. Grampian Region

Classification
Highland (Speyside)

Origins and background
This distillery was built originally in 1885 by James Stuart and was then known as the Mills of Rothes with the intention of milling cereals, but he found that whisky distilling was more profitable and converted the operation. However his heart does not seem to have been in it for two years later he sold out to the Gilbey brothers, Walter and Alfred, who although starting out as wine merchants and progressing to gin distilling had early on appreciated the potential of whisky distilling. Now part of International Distillers and Vintners Ltd, since 1962, the distillery has a capacity of 750,000 proof gallons, almost all of which goes for blending, although some no doubt forms part of the vatted malt Strathspey marketed by the parent company. It used to add the Glenlivet affix, but this has now been dropped. Only a limited quantity is bottled.

Owned by
International Distillers & Vintners Ltd

Visitors
By arrangement. Tel: 05422 2531

Age and strength when bottled
12 years at 40% volume

Comments
Bottled at 12 years and 40% volume this malt whisky is clearly from Speyside, making a pleasant very smooth pre-prandial dram.

GLENALLACHIE

Situation
Aberlour, Banffshire. Grampian Region

Classification
Highland (Speyside)

Origins and background
This distillery was built in the mini-boom years of the 1960s. The architect who designed it, Mr Delme Evans, also designed two others, one on the Isle of Jura above Islay and the other at Tullibardine in Perthshire. It can be no coincidence that Glenallachie and Isle of Jura were both then owned by Scottish and Newcastle Breweries Ltd, who obviously liked his work on their Isle of Jura distillery in 1958. Taken over in 1985 by Invergordon Distillers and then temporarily closed it was acquired later by Pernod Ricard.

Owned by
Ricard International SA

Visitors
By arrangement

Age and strength when bottled
12 years at 40% volume

Comments
A pleasing smooth light dram which is best drunk before dinner when the subtle fragrance of the aftermath can be fully savoured.

GLENBURGIE

Situation
Forres, Morayshire. Grampian Region

Classification
Highland (Speyside)

Origins and background
This is another distillery which can lay claims to being among the oldest in the Highlands since it is said to have been established in 1810 by William Paul with a modest capacity of 90 gallons. It changed hands a number of times during the 19th century and each change of ownership appears to have resulted in an increase in its capacity so that when it was taken over by Alexander Fraser & Co. in the 1890s the wash still had a capacity of 1,500 gallons. The distillery was subsequently acquired by James & George Stodart Ltd of Dumbarton, who were themselves taken over by Hiram Walker (Scotland) Ltd, in 1930, in their first venture into the Scotch Whisky industry. Two spirit stills and two wash-stills were also added in 1958, but removed in 1980. For a while the whisky produced from them was known as Glencraig. Any malt whisky bottled is marketed as Glenburgie-Glenlivet.

Owned by
Allied Distillers Ltd

Visitors
By arrangement. Tel: 03438 5258

Age and strength when bottled
5 years at 40% volume

Comments
It is only occasionally bottled by the distillery, but is obtainable from the independent bottlers. It is a fairly typical light Speyside malt whisky and as such a good dram. It is notable that although twenty miles from Glenlivet the firm still finds the use of the hyphenated Glenlivet affix worthwhile.

GLENCADAM

Situation
Brechin, Angus. Tayside Region

Classification
Highland (Eastern)

Origins and background
Situated in a steep-sided glen the distillery obtains ample
water supplies from the Moorfoot Loch. It was first licensed
in 1825 and as with many around this date was almost
certainly built on the site of a previously illicit still. It went
through a number of changes of ownership until acquired
in 1891 by Gilmour Thomson & Co. Ltd. The distillery was
finally bought by Hiram Walker and Sons (Scotland) Ltd in
1954, as another acquisition in their expanding empire. The
whisky almost all goes for blending, but may be obtained
from the independent bottlers.

Owned by
Allied Distillers Ltd

Visitors
By arrangement. Tel: 03562 2217

Age and strength when bottled
Varies as only obtainable from the independent bottlers.

Comments
On a sample tasted aged 14 years and 46% it would seem
to be a good after-dinner malt worth while bottling by the
distillery.

GLENDRONACH

Situation
Forgue, by Huntly, Aberdeenshire. Grampian Region

Classification
Highland (Speyside)

Origins and background
The distillery was built in 1826 by James Allardyce and a
syndicate of local businessmen. Unfortunately disagree-
ments and financial losses through mismanagement in
the early years were followed by an extensive fire in 1837
after which the distillery was taken over by Mr Walter
Scott. Its history thereafter was fairly straightforward. It
takes its name and water from the Dronac burn. It was
acquired by Captain Charles Grant, one of the Grants
of the Glenfiddich distilling family, until it was sold
to William Teacher & Sons Ltd in 1960, when it was
considerably enlarged. It retained certain old-fashioned
features such as floor maltings and coal-fired pot-stills,
but was extensively modernised. Until then it had used
the hyphenated Glenlivet prefix, but this was dropped.
Local control is in the hands of the Glendronach Distillery
Company Limited, Huntly, and comparatively recently
production has doubled.

Owned by
Allied Distillers Ltd

Visitors
Reception centre. Tel: 046682 202

Age and strength when bottled
12 years at 40% volume

Comments
Comes as the Original, aged in oak and sherry wood casks,
or the Sherrywood, aged in sherry wood casks. Favoured
in Aberdeenshire. The Original is a touch peppery initially,
but both are good after-dinner drams with a distinctive
long dry aftermath.

GLENDULLAN

Situation
Dufftown, Banffshire. Grampian Region

Classification
Highland (Speyside)

Origins and background
This distillery was built by William Williams & Sons Ltd
of Aberdeen at the height of the whisky boom in 1896 at
Dufftown making the seventh distillery ringing the town.
William Williams & Sons Ltd were whisky blenders and
merchants who used most of the malt whisky produced
at Glendullan for their blends, although some was bottled
as a malt whisky of sufficient distinction to acquire a Royal
Warrant in 1902 as supplied to King Edward VII. During
the 1914-18 War they merged with Macdonald Greenlees
and formed Macdonald Greenlees and Williams (Distillers) Ltd, being subsequently acquired by the DCL. At
one time the hyphenated Glenlivet addition to the name
was used and it was marketed as Glendullan-Glenlivet, but
this practice has now ceased.

Owned by
United Distillers

Visitors
Reception centre. Tel: 0340 20250

Age and strength when bottled
12 years at 43% volume

Comments
A smooth dram with a good aftermath this makes a good
after-dinner Speyside malt whisky which deserves to be
better known.

GLENESK

Situation
Hillside, Montrose, Angus. Grampian Region

Classification
Highland (Eastern)

Origins and background
This distillery has changed its name more often than most.
It was built in 1897 at the height of the whisky boom by a
firm with the unlikely name of Septimus Parsonage & Co.
Ltd. It was then known as the Highland Esk Distillery. It
was soon acquired by a firm of distillers called Heddle
and was renamed the North Esk. It was damaged by
fire in 1910, but rebuilt, only to be closed during the
1914-18 War. After the war in 1919 it was acquired by
Thomas Bernard & Co. and used as a maltings. In 1938
it was bought by Associated Scottish Distilleries Ltd, and
turned into a patent-still grain distillery, known as the
Montrose Distillery. In 1954 it was acquired by the DCL
and returned once more to malt whisky distilling in 1965,
at this stage being re-named Hillside. Finally in 1980 the
name was once more changed to Glenesk. The whisky is
mostly used for blending but is also bottled at 12 years. It
is currently closed.

Owned by
United Distillers

Visitors
By arrangement

Age and strength when bottled
12 years at 40% volume

Comments
A sound faintly sweetish after-dinner dram with a clean
dry aftermath.

GLENFARCLAS

Situation
Marypark, Ballindalloch, Banffshire. Grampian Region

Classification
Highland (Speyside)

Origins and background
Built in 1836 by Robert Hay this distillery was purchased
in 1865 by John Grant, the first of five generations of the
Grant family who have owned the distillery. Initially he
sub-let the distillery to John Smith, the noted distiller at
the nearby Glenlivet Distillery, who already had established a notable reputation. It is not surprising therefore
that the affix Glenlivet was added on to the Glenfarclas
name. John Grant took over full control of the distillery
in 1870. During the 1880s he handed over increasing
control to his son George, and died in 1889. George
unfortunately died prematurely in 1890 when his wife
took over control and managed the business successfully
until their sons, John and George, were old enough to
take over themselves in 1895. In that year they formed
The Glenfarclas-Glenlivet Distillery Co. Ltd, on an equal
share basis with the Leith blenders Pattison, Elder & Co.,
whose spectacular bankruptcy in 1898 signalled the end
of the whisky boom. Thereafter the Grant family remained
in full control of the distillery. John Grant retired from the
partnership after the 1914-18 War, but George remained
in sole control until 1947 when he formed J.& G. Grant
Ltd. On his death in 1949 the distillery went to his sons
George Scott Grant and John P. Grant. The latter died in
1960, but the family remains in control of the distillery.
As one of his first actions in 1896 at the height of the
whisky boom George Grant had instituted considerable
rebuilding and renovations which brought the production up to nearly 300,000 proof gallons a year, or 778,500
litres of alcohol. It is indicative of the long depression in
the industry that it was not until 1960 that considerable
rebuilding and modernisation finally doubled the capacity to 600,000 gallons, or 1,557,000 litres of alcohol. Since

then the annual capacity has been raised yet again to a million gallons, or 2.595 million litres of alcohol. Clearly finding no need for it any longer the Glenfarclas Distillery has now dropped the affix Glenlivet and reverted to its original name.

Owned by
J. & G. Grant Ltd

Visitors
Reception centre – On the Whisky Trail. Tel: 08072 257

Age and strength when bottled
8 years at 40% and 60% volume; 12 years at 43% volume; 15 years at 46% volume; 21 years at 43% volume

Comments
With nearly 125 years of the same family in control this must be unique even in an industry where tradition and continuity counts for a great deal. This is a malt whisky of character and Glenfarclas makes a very fine after-dinner dram at any age and strength.

GLENFIDDICH

Situation
Dufftown, Banffshire. Grampian Region

Classification
Highland (Speyside)

Origins and background
The founding of this distillery, like that of Glenfarclas, is very much a family story relating yet again to the name Grant, itself amongst the most notable and frequently found wherever Scotch whisky is distilled. Although starting some twenty years after the Grants of Glenfarclas the Grants of Glenfiddich made up for matters by sheer numbers. In 1886 William Grant who already had twenty years experience of distilling in the Mortlach distillery bought the land on the Robbie Dubh spring nearby. He also bought the old disused plant from the Cardow distillery which was then being re-equipped for £120 and set about building his own distillery, using water for cooling purposes from the nearby Fiddich burn from which the distillery gained its name of Glenfiddich. With the aid of his seven sons and his entire capital of £755 he had the distillery producing whisky by 1887 and was so successful that in five years he was building Balvenie close at hand. Thereafter expansion was steady with the formation of a limited company William Grant & Sons Ltd in 1903 with which William Grant remained actively involved until his death in 1923. Meanwhile Captain Charles Grant one of his sons had taken over the Glendronach distillery (sold to William Teacher in 1960, see Glendronach) and in the post 1939-45 boom years the firm, still very much a family concern, built a grain distillery at Girvan in Ayrshire, near which they built a Lowland malt distillery named Ladyburn used entirely for blending. The success of their blend Grant's Standfast, which owed much to skilful marketing was followed in the 1960s by the widespread foreign sales and marketing of the Glenfiddich, the first determinedly successful overseas sales of a malt whisky, gaining a Queen's Award to Industry for Export

Achievement in 1974. Still very much a family company William Grant & Sons Ltd continue to manage Glenfiddich and the neighbouring Balvenie distilleries as well as the Girvan plant and their worldwide blending and marketing projects with determination and flair, while Grants are still prominent in the board of directors, the grandsons and great grandsons of William and his progeny. It is a remarkable success story by any standards.

Owned by
William Grant & Sons Ltd

Visitors
Reception centre – On the Whisky Trail. Tel: 03402 0373

Age and strength when bottled
No age given at 40% volume: 18, 21 and 30 years at 43% volume.

Comments
With their widespread overseas sales and their reception centre at Glenfiddich distillery the former must be amongst the malt whiskies most frequently drunk for the first time. At least 8 years old, it makes a good light introduction to malt whisky which should interest and encourage those who have not drunk any previously. Also available at 18, 21 and 30 years old at 43% volume and improves with each. With the latter two a presentation decanter is included.

GLENGLASSAUGH

Situation
Portsoy, Banffshire. Grampian Region

Classification
Highland (Speyside)

Origins and background
This distillery was built in 1875 about a couple of miles along the coast from the small fishing village of Portsoy, six and a half miles west of Banff itself. It obtains its water from local springs close to the site. The Highland Distilleries acquired it in 1892 and still own it. They completely rebuilt and renovated it in 1959 so that it now has an output of 1.2 million litres of alcohol. Almost all of this is used for blending but some is bottled by the distillery and the independent bottlers.

Owned by
The Highland Distilleries Co. plc

Visitors
Reception centre. Tel: 041 332 7511

Age and strength when bottled
12 years at 40% volume

Comments
This is a pleasant slightly sweetish dram but with a dry aftermath which deserves to be more easily available.

GLENGOYNE

Situation
Dumgoyne, Stirlingshire (2 miles S.E. of Killearn). Tayside Region

Classification
Highland (South West)

Origins and background
Sited in a wooded glen at the foot of Dumgoyne Hill, the water supply comes from the nearby Campsie Fells. This is a particularly attractively placed distillery and is also a very suitable one for visitors who want to see the whole process without too much walking. It is also very convenient for Glasgow. First licensed to Archibald McLellan in 1833 it was then known as the Glenguin distillery. When it was taken over by the brothers Alexander and Gavin Lang in 1876 it was re-named the Glengoyne distillery. Lang Brothers Ltd were themselves taken over by Robertson & Baxter Ltd in 1965 and the distillery was then completely modernised.

Owned by
Lang Brothers Ltd

Visitors
Reception centre. Tel: 041 332 6361

Age and strength when bottled
10 years at 40% volume; 12 and 17 years at 43% volume

Comments
Situated right on the imaginary Highland Line it may be classified as a Southern Highland malt whisky, but regardless of position the ten year old is a light, clean and pleasant dram. The 12 year old is rather more mature and smoother and the 17 year old even more so. In effect it changes with age from a good pre-dinner dram to a good after-dinner dram.

GLENKINCHIE

Situation
Glenkinchie, Pencaitland, East Lothian. Lothian Region

Classification
Lowland (East)

Origins and background
Built somewhere around 1837 by a local farmer named
John Rate it was subsequently sold to another East Lothian
farmer named Christie, who bought it not for distilling,
but for use as a saw mill and cattle shed. In 1880 it was
sold again to a syndicate interested in turning it back
into a distillery. In 1890, as the whisky boom developed,
they formed the Glenkinchie Distillery Company. In 1914
it was taken over by the Scottish Malt Distillers Ltd, since
when it has been considerably modernised and rebuilt.
Most of the whisky goes for blending, but some is bottled
independently and some has recently been bottled by the
distillery itself.

Owned by
United Distillers

Visitors
Reception centre and museum. Tel: 0875340 333. Popular
as the nearest to Edinburgh.

Age and strength when bottled
10 years old and 43% volume when bottled by the distillery.

Comments
There is an attractive dryness about this distinctively
Lowland malt whisky, making a good clean dram with
a smooth aftermath. Fortunately it is now more widely
available.

THE GLENLIVET

Situation
Minmore, Banffshire. Grampian Region

Classification
Highland (Speyside)

Origins and background
It is well known that George Smith founded the Glenlivet
Distillery in 1824. His ancestors appear to have been
first recorded in that then wild and desolate area of the
Highlands in 1715 at the time of the first Jacobite rising.
Although Thomas Smith, George's great grandfather, was
probably out with his Laird in the 1715 rebellion he does
not appear to have supported the Jacobites in the 1745 Rising. It may have been because of this that he and his family
appear to have escaped any of the draconian punishments
imposed by the Duke of Cumberland after the '45.

By the time Thomas' great grandson, George Smith, took
over from his father Andrew in 1817 at Upper Drumin
as one of the Duke of Gordon's tenants illicit 'Glenlivet'
whisky was known and popular as far south as Edinburgh.
It was George who first took out a license in 1824 under the
Act of 1823 with the Duke's encouragement and started
distilling legally in the face of fierce opposition from his
erstwhile friends who still continued to distil illicitly. It
was thus in 1824 that the distillery at Upper Drumin
was amongst the first distilleries to distil legally with
a capacity of fifty gallons weekly which by 1839 had
risen dramatically four times to 200 gallons a week. With
his son-in-law Captain William Grant distilling at nearby
Auchorachan, George Smith maintained that only they
could distil whisky with the title Glenlivet, but in 1850
William Grant died and his distillery ceased operations.
However George Smith then built another distillery at
Delnabo near Tomintoul.

By 1858 George and his son John Gordon Smith had
built a much larger distillery at Minmore and closed
down both Delnabo and Upper Drumin. The new distillery had a capacity of 600 gallons a week and as a

result of the energy of their agent Andrew Usher the production was soon heavily in demand and in 1864 being exported abroad. In 1871 John Gordon Smith inherited the distillery on his father's death. In 1880 he established by due process of law that no-one else was legally entitled to the use of the name The Glenlivet, but all others must use a prefix. John Gordon Smith was succeeded in 1901 by his nephew George Smith Grant, son of Captain William Grant of Auchorachan.

In 1921 the distillery went to Captain W. H. Smith Grant his younger son. In 1952 George and J. G. Smith Ltd merged with J. & J. Grant, Glen Grant Distillery forming the Glenlivet and Glen Grant Distilleries Ltd. In 1970 they merged yet again with the noted blenders Hill Thomson & Co. Ltd and Longmorn-Glenlivet Distilleries Ltd when the name of the merged companies was rationalised to The Glenlivet Distillers Ltd. In 1978 their long record of independence came to an end with their acquisition by Seagram Distillers plc.

Owned by
The Seagram Co. Ltd

Visitors
Reception centre. Tel: 08073 427

Age and strength when bottled
12 years at 40% volume

Comments
There is an understandable, if deplorable, tendency for Seagram Distillers to reduce the independence and long-standing reputation of the product of this company to just one item in their extensive, if notable, drinks portfolio. Although still an excellent and outstanding malt whisky there is perhaps already a suspicion of a blander style becoming more apparent than in the past. They should leave well alone.

GLENLOCHY

Situation
Fort William, Inverness-shire. Highland Region

Classification
Highland (Western)

Origins and background
Originating in 1898 this was a very late speculative venture at the extreme end of the whisky boom by a hopeful native of Nairn, Mr David McAndie. It had hardly begun operations before the boom was over and hard times had started. Thereafter there were two long periods of forced closure before it was bought in 1937 by Train & McIntyre Ltd, and run by them through their subsidiary Associated Scottish Distilleries Ltd. Finally in 1953 when DCL took over Train & McIntyre Ltd, it became a DCL subsidiary. It was closed again permanently in 1983 and has now been dismantled.

Owned by
United Distillers

Visitors
No

Age and strength when bottled
Only bottled by the independent bottlers

Comments
To judge by the sample tasted a very light but pleasantly peaty pre-dinner dram. Very little more is likely to be available.

GLENLOSSIE

Situation
Elgin, Morayshire. Grampian Region

Classification
Highland (Speyside)

Origins and background
This distillery was built in 1876 at Thomshill, about three miles south of Elgin It was founded by a syndicate of three formed by a local hotel owner John Duff. When the partnership changed in 1896 it was agreed to form The Glenlossie-Glenlivet Distillery Co. Ltd. Considerable development throughout the following months including a private railway line to Longmorn Station and a new warehouse resulted in the company going public in 1897. The effects of the recession in the Scotch Whisky industry during the ensuing years, however, resulted in the Scottish Malt Distillers Ltd taking them over in 1919. In 1930 the company was dissolved and the distillery became part of Scottish Malt Distillers Ltd. The bulk goes for blending and none is bottled by the distillery.

Owned by
United Distillers

Visitors
Reception centre. Tel: 03438 577

Age and strength when bottled
Only available from the independent bottlers.

Comments
At 18 years and 46% volume, scarcely surprisingly, the sample tried tasted smooth and mellow. It certainly seemed as if it would merit bottling in its own right.

GLENMORANGIE *(glen morange-y)*

Situation
Tain, Ross-shire. Highland Region

Classification
Highland (Northern)

Origins and background
Overlooking the Dornoch Firth near the town of Tain, it is claimed that brewing and distilling has been carried on at or around this site since the Middle Ages. The present distillery, however, only dates from 1843 when William Matheson and his brother converted the brewery operating there into a distillery. Its name derives from the Morangie burn which runs through a small glen beside it. It obtains its water from a spring rich in minerals from which the brewers who preceded them had taken water for their ale then renowned as far south as Inverness. In 1893 a private siding connected the distillery to the main railway line which not only improved the transport of whisky to the south, but also made it easier to obtain supplies of local peat until these were exhausted. It was here that the use of steam coils in the stills to separate the alcohol from the wash to avoid affecting the whisky's flavour was initiated and subsequently copied by a number of others in the Highlands. In 1918 the distillery was acquired by Macdonald & Muir Ltd and now produces about 600,000 gallons a year, mostly bottled at 10 years.

Owned by
Macdonald Martin Distilleries plc

Visitors
Reception centre. Tel: 0862 2043

Age and strength when bottled
10 years at 40% volume

Comments
A distinctive and very smooth pre-dinner dram which is also mellow enough to be drunk with pleasure after a meal. Well known and deservedly well liked.

GLENORDIE *see* ORD

GLENROTHES

Situation
Rothes, Morayshire. Grampian Region

Classification
Highland (Speyside)

Origins and background
The distillery was built on the site of an old sawmill in
1878 by a syndicate of Rothes and Elgin businessmen. It
went into production in 1879 and eight years later in 1887
merged with the Islay Distillery Co. to form the Highland
Distillers Co. Ltd. Since then there has been periodic
extensive renovation and re-building. A comparatively
recently completed still-house has two new pairs of stills
giving a capacity overall of around 5.3 million litres of
spirit. Almost all goes for blending and only a little is
bottled through the independent bottlers.

Owned by
The Highland Distilleries Co. plc

Visitors
Reception centre. Tel: 03438 0331

Age and strength when bottled
Only by the independent bottlers

Comments
The sample tasted at 8 years and 40% volume seemed a
good dry dram with a pleasing aftermath and well worth
bottling in its own right.

GLENTAUCHERS

Situation
Mulben, Banffshire. Grampian Region

Classification
Highland (Speyside)

Origins and background
This distillery was built by James Buchanan, promoter of the famed 'Black and White' blend and prominent amongst the 'Big Five' of the late 19th century whisky boom. Although primarily a skilful salesman and promoter of blended whiskies he naturally became involved in the power struggle between the grain whisky and the pot-still malt whisky distillers. However he decided in 1898 that he needed his own supplies of malt whisky and built this distillery at Glentauchers in association with his Glaswegian whisky broker W. P. Lowrie. The controlling company was named the Glentauchers-Glenlivet Distillery Co. Ltd, which in 1906, on W. P. Lowrie's retirement, was taken over by James Buchanan & Co. Ltd. In due course in 1925 the distillery became part of the DCL empire. The malt whisky has from time to time been bottled at 5 and 12 years old, but is now only available from the independent bottlers. Mostly used for blending it was closed in 1985, but since its acquisition by Allied Distillers in 1989 is to be re-opened.

Owned by
Allied Distillers Ltd

Visitors
By arrangement

Age and strength when bottled
Only bottled by the independent bottlers

Comments
A 20 year old at 46% volume seemed to be a very light and dry pre-dinner malt but possibly too long in the cask. It will be interesting to taste this from the distillery again in the late 1990s.

GLENTURRET

Situation
Crieff, Perthshire. Highland Region

Classification
Highland (South)

Origins and background
Glenturret claims to be amongst the oldest distilleries in Scotland on the grounds that illicit distilling had been taking place on the site prior to the establishment of the first distillery in 1775. It is well placed between two hills on the banks of the Turret water providing a good water supply. In the nature of things the distillery also had a succession of proprietors, prominent amongst whom appears to have been a Crieff landowner Thomas Stewart. In 1959 Mr James Fairlie took over as Managing Director and Distiller and a steady programme of renovation and rebuilding was set in motion. By 1977 the distillery had a capacity of around 175,000 proof gallons, and in 1974 Glenturret was awarded a Gold Seal in the International Wines and Spirit competition for the best bottled matured malt under 12 years old. Projected annual capacity should already have passed the 375,000 proof gallons mark. In 1981 Glenturret Distillery Ltd, was taken over by Cointreau SA, the French liqueur makers, but although most goes for blending a certain amount is bottled at varying ages.

Owned by
Cointreau SA

Visitors
Reception centre. Tel: 0764-2424.

Age and strength when bottled
8, 12, 15 and 21 years at 43% volume

Comments
This is an unusual but sound malt whisky with a full smooth flavour suitable for an after-dinner dram, which improves considerably with age. They appreciate the value of publicity and of producing their own malt whisky.

GLENURY ROYAL

Situation
Stonehaven, Kincardineshire. Grampian Region

Classification
Highland (Eastern)

Origins and background
The distillery was built in 1836 by Captain Robert Barclay of Ury, MP for Kincardine and a prominent local farmer and landowner as well as a remarkable athlete renowned for his ability as a long-distance walker. The distillery is situated on the north side of the river Cowie a short distance outside Stonehaven and in the district of Ury from which the glen in which it is placed and the distillery itself get their name. On Captain Barclay's death in 1854 it was not long before the distillery passed to William Ritchie & Co. of Glasgow who retained it until 1937 when it was sold to the Glenury Distillery Ltd. In 1938 it was again sold to Associated Scottish Distilleries Ltd, a subsidiary of Train & McIntyre Ltd, themselves a subsidiary for the National Distillers of America for whom Joseph Hobbs of Great Glen Ranch fame was acting as purchasing agent. In 1953 DCL acquired Train & McIntyre Ltd and the distillery came under their control, being licensed by them to John Gillon & Co. Ltd. Although the bulk goes for blending some was bottled by the distillery at 12 years and 40% volume. The distillery has been closed since 1985.

Owned by
United Distillers

Visitors
Only by arrangement

Age and strength when bottled
12 years at 40% volume

Comments
A good light and dry pre-dinner dram with a pleasing slightly peaty aftermath. Since the closure of Glenugie it is now the most easterly distillery in Scotland and the malt whisky should be readily marketable as such.

HIGHLAND PARK

Situation
Kirkwall, Orkney

Classification
Island (Orkney)

Origins and background
The distillery is built on a hill overlooking Kirkwall on the site of the bothy of an illicit distiller named Magnus Eunson who started distilling there in the eighteenth century. He was an unprincipled rogue who took advantage of his position as a church officer to evade capture of his illicit whisky by hiding it under the pulpit. The early history of the distillery is vague, but it is said to have been started legally by David Robertson around 1789. In 1888 James Grant, whose father had been the chief distiller and manager of the Glenlivet Distillery, became managing partner and in 1895 he acquired full control. The Grant family retained control until 1937 when the distillery was acquired by Highland Distilleries Ltd. The distillery has its own maltings although barley has to be imported from the mainland. The water supply comes from two local wells. The Orkney peat used has a distinctive aroma and a small quantity of heather is burnt with it, which may account for the distinctive flavour of this very fine malt whisky from the most northerly distillery in Scotland.

Owned by
The Highland Distilleries Co. plc

Visitors
Reception centre. Tel: 0856 3107

Age and strength when bottled
12 years at 40% volume

Comments
This has to be acknowledged as one of the finest after-dinner drams. It is smooth and full of character with a fine aftermath and, although recently altered, the distinctively shaped bottle is still a welcome sight.

IMPERIAL

Situation
Carron, Morayshire. Grampian Region

Classification
Highland (Speyside)

Origins and background
The distillery was established in 1887 by Thomas Mackenzie, who already owned Daluaine and the Talisker Distilleries. He incorporated all three distilleries in 1898 as the Daluaine-Talisker Distilleries Ltd. In 1916 the company was acquired jointly by Dewar, DCL, W. P. Lowrie and Johnnie Walker, thus ending up as part of the DCL in 1925, the year of the great mergers into DCL. The product all went for blending except for some bottled independently. Acquired in 1989 by Allied Distillers Ltd.

Owned by
Allied Distillers Ltd

Visitors
By arrangement

Age and strength when bottled
Only bottled by the independent bottlers

Comments
On one sample this seems to be well worth bottling as an interesting after-dinner dram and now probably will be.

INCHGOWER

Situation
Buckie, Banffshire. Grampian Region

Classification
Highland (Speyside)

Origins and background
Originally established in 1824 as Tochineal Distillery close to Cullen by Alexander Wilson the distillery was moved in 1871 by Alexander Wilson & Co. to Rathven a small village about one and a half miles east of Buckie to ensure a ready supply of water from the Letter Burn and the springs at Aultmoor. At some point it was acquired and run by Buckie Town Council, but its period of municipal ownership ended when it was acquired by A. K. Bell in 1936 on behalf of Arthur Bell & Sons, now themselves acquired by Guinness plc, and merged with DCL as United Distillers plc.

Owned by
United Distillers

Visitors
Reception centre. Tel: 0542 31161

Age and strength when bottled
12 years at 40% volume

Comments
A medium light malt with a touch of sweetness making a pleasant distinctive dram.

INCHMURRIN *see* LOCH LOMOND:

INVERLEVEN

Situation
Dumbarton, Strathclyde. Strathclyde Region

Classification
Lowland (Northern)

Origins and background
This distillery was established in 1938 as, in effect, a malt whisky distilling complex since it stands alongside the Lomond distillery and adjacent to the Hiram Walker Dumbarton Grain distillery. It is situated right on the imaginary 'Highland Line', but is classified as a Lowland malt. It obtains its water from the River Leven and Lochs Lomond and Humphrey. The production is used almost entirely for blending by Hiram Walker but it has in the past been occasionally bottled by the Lomond distillery. Since 1988 part of Allied Distillers Ltd.

Owned by
Allied Distillers Ltd

Visitors
By arrangement

Age and strength when bottled
Only obtainable through the independent distillers

Comments
Although it could really just as well be classified as western highland this tastes more like a Lowland malt whisky. It is a light and slightly sweet dram with a dry aftermath.

ISLE OF JURA

Situation
Craighouse, Isle of Jura, Argyll. Strathclyde Region

Classification
Island (Jura)

Origins and background
It is claimed there was distilling on the site of the present
distillery at Craighouse as early as the seventeenth century
and that illicit distilling was carried out in a cave nearby,
but the present distillery only dates from around 1810. The
buildings were owned by the Campbells, landlords of the
Jura estate, but the stills and equipment belonged to James
Ferguson who operated the distillery for his own profit.
This arrangement ceased in 1901 when the parties to it
quarrelled and Ferguson removed his equipment and the
landlords removed the roof of the building to avoid the
payment of rates. In 1958 Mr Riley-Smith and Mr Fletcher,
two landowners on the island, approached Scottish and
Newcastle Breweries with a proposal for rebuilding the
distillery to bring fresh employment to Jura. The distillery
was built by Charles Mackinlay & Co. Ltd, a subsidiary of
Scottish & Newcastle Breweries Ltd, to the design of Mr
Delmé Morgan and went into production in 1963 under
the name of the Isle of Jura Distillery Co. Ltd. It has since
been acquired by Invergordon Distillers Ltd.

Owned by
Invergordon Distillers Ltd

Visitors
Reception centre. Tel: 049682 240

Age and strength when bottled
10 years at 40% volume

Comments
Although just north of Islay this much more resembles a
Highland malt whisky than an Islay malt. It is a pleasant
smooth, light bodied and clean tasting dram.

KNOCKANDO

Situation
Knockando, Morayshire. Grampian Region

Classification
Highland (Speyside)

Origins and background
The distillery was built by Ian Thompson at the end of the
whisky boom and only went into small scale production
for a couple of years before closing down and falling into
disrepair but in 1904 it was bought cheaply by W. & A.
Gilbey. The Gaelic meaning of the name is 'little black
hill' and it is in a good position above the Spey with a
good water supply. The distillery has a capacity of 500,000
gallons and is now owned by International Distillers &
Vintners. While most of the production goes for blending
a certain amount is bottled by the distillery.

Owned by
The International Distillers & Vintners Ltd

Visitors
Reception centre. Tel: 03406 205

Age and strength when bottled
Generally from around 11 to 13 years

Comments
This is a light and smooth after-dinner dram with a
good distinctive aftermath. It is a pleasing Speyside malt
whisky, bottled when considered at its best by the distillery manager. The dates of distilling and bottling are on
the label.

KNOCKDHU *(nokdoo)*

Situation
Knock, Banffshire. Grampian Region

Classification
Highland (Speyside)

Origins and background
Knockdhu stands above the small river Isla from which
it draws its water. It was built in 1893 and is of historic
interest in that it was the first malt whisky distillery to be
built by the DCL. All its production was used for blending,
but some was occasionally available as a malt whisky from
the independent bottlers. The distillery was closed in 1983
during the recession in the industry, but it is a sign of the
times that it was acquired in 1988 by Inver House Distillers
Ltd, and re-started distilling in 1989. At present however
only available through the independent bottlers.

Owned by
Inver House Distillers Ltd

Visitors
Welcome. Tel: 046686 223

Age and strength when bottled
Only through independent bottlers

Comments
It seems to be a medium dry after-dinner dram with a good
aftermath.

LADYBURN

Situation
Girvan, Ayrshire. Dumfries & Galloway Region

Classification
Lowland (South West)

Origins and background
Post 1939-45 War expansion caused William Grant & Sons
Ltd to build a new grain distillery at Girvan in Ayrshire
in 1963 with a ready water supply obtained from the
Penwhapple Loch. In 1965 they went on to build the
Ladyburn Lowland malt distillery adjacent to it and with
the same water supply. In 1975 the malt distillery was
dismantled and only the grain distillery left. The entire
production was used for blending but occasionally some
may be bottled by the independent bottlers.

Owned by
William Grant & Sons Ltd

Visitors
By arrangement

Age and strength when bottled
Only bottled by the independent bottlers

Comments
Only tasted as a 20 year old at 46% volume, but as it was
bottled independently little of value can be said except
that perhaps it is understandable why it was only used
for blending.

LAGAVULIN *(lag-avoolin)*

Situation
Port Ellen, Islay, Argyll. Strathclyde Region

Classification
Islay (Island West Coast)

Origins and background
The Gaelic meaning of Lagavulin is 'the mill in the valley' and the distillery claims to date as far back as 1742, but the modern distillery was probably built nearer 1824. It is built close beside the village of Lagavulin in a small bay with its own jetty and obtains its water from the lochs in the hill of Solan. There were a number of owners in the 19th century, but the Grahams went into partnership with James Logan Mackie, uncle of the famous Peter Mackie, who was to become prominent amongst the 'Big Five' in the late 19th century. It was at Lagavulin that Peter Mackie learned his craft as a distiller and on his uncle's death in the late 1880s he inherited the distillery. The whisky was used as the basis for his famous 'White Horse' blend on which his subsequent reputation was founded. When DCL took over Mackie & Co., Distillers, Ltd., after his death in 1927 they changed the name to White Horse Distillers Ltd, one of the few examples of a company being named after a blend rather than vice-versa. The bulk of the production still goes for blending but some is bottled by the distillery.

Owned by
United Distillers

Visitors
Reception centre. Tel 0496 2400

Age and strength when bottled
16 years at 43% volume

Comments
A full-bodied malt whisky with a powerful iodine flavour and aftermath it has all the distinctive Islay character. Considered by many to be the most distinctive of the Islay malt whiskies it has a notable smoothness making a memorable dram.

LAPHROAIG *(la-froig)*

Situation
Port Ellen, Islay, Argyll. Strathclyde Region

Classification
Islay (Island West Coast)

Origins and background
About one mile from Port Ellen this distillery is in a most attractive position set on a small bay protected by rocky islets. It was built around 1820, operated illicitly, by two brothers, Donald and Alexander Johnston. Donald Johnston took over sole control in 1836, by which time the distillery was licensed and legal. Ownership passed through the family until in 1928 Ian Hunter became sole owner. In 1950 he formed a private limited company D. Johnston & Co. Ltd with a Miss E. L. Williamson (later Mrs Campbell) as Secretary and Director. On his death in 1954 she took over his post of Managing Director. When the company was acquired by Long John International Ltd, acting for Seager Evans & Co. in 1967 she continued as Chairman and Director until her death in 1972, a rare example of a female in charge of what is largely a male preserve. Much of the whisky goes to make the notable blend Islay Mist, but fortunately some is bottled by the distillery, now acquired by Allied Distillers Ltd.

Owned by
Allied Distillers Ltd

Visitors
Welcome by appointment. Tel: 0496 2418

Age and strength when bottled
10 and 15 years at 40% volume

Comments
A very distinctively Islay dram, slightly sweeter and not as full bodied as Lagavulin, but possibly none the worse of that. The 15 year old is drier and more full bodied, but at either age like Lagavulin this is a malt whisky about which strong views are held both for and against.

LEDAIG *see* TOBERMORY

LINKWOOD

Situation
Elgin, Morayshire. Grampian Region

Classification
Highland (Speyside)

Origins and background
Standing just a mile outside Elgin in wooded surround-
ings this distillery was originally established by Peter
Brown in 1821. It was named after the old mansion
house which it replaced. The distillery was largely rebuilt
by his son William Brown in 1873. Control was passed to
the Linkwood-Glenlivet Distillery Ltd, in 1896. For thirty
years from 1902 until 1932 the company was managed
by a Mr Innes Cameron, who established its reputation
as producing a sound malt whisky. On his death the
distillery was acquired by the DCL. It is still produced
as a malt whisky, although much goes for blending.

Owned by
United Distillers

Visitors
Reception centre. Tel: 0343 7004

Age and strength when bottled
12 years at 40% volume

Comments
A very much under-rated malt whisky this is a very good,
slightly peaty and very clean tasting Speyside dram with a
good aftermath well worth drinking at any time.

LITTLEMILL

Situation
Bowling, Dunbartonshire. Strathclyde Region

Classification
Lowland (Western)

Origins and background
This is generally believed to be amongst the oldest distilleries in Scotland, but its exact origins are uncertain to say the least. It is thought that as far back as 1750 a Glasgow maltster, George Buchanan, purchased the estate of Auchterlonie, which included the site of Littlemill. When distilling as opposed to brewing started it is impossible to say. The probability is that the present distillery dates from around 1800, but there were numerous owners until a Duncan G. Thomas, a US citizen, took it over in 1931 and formed the Littlemill Distillery Co. Ltd. In 1959 Barton Brands Inc. of Chicago became shareholders and in 1971 bought out D. G. Thomas and took over control forming Barton Distilling (Scotland) Ltd. In 1982 Amalgamated Distilled Products plc acquired control of Barton Brands Inc. and now own the distillery. Since it uses highland peat and water from the Kilpatrick hills this might be regarded as a borderline case, but it is rightly classified as Lowland. It was briefly closed in 1987 but re-opened the following year. Most of the whisky is used for blending, but some is bottled by the distillery.

Owned by
Barton International Ltd

Visitors
By arrangement. Tel: 03879 4154

Age and strength when bottled
8 years at 40% volume

Comments
A light and rather pleasing smooth pre-dinner dram. It was bottled at 5 and 8 years but the 8 year old was very much superior and the 5 year old has now been discontinued.

LOCH LOMOND

Situation
Alexandria. Strathclyde Region

Classification
Highland (South Western)

Origins and background
Located at Alexandria, close to Loch Lomond, from which it takes its name, the distillery was built on the site of an old printing and bleach works. It was also built almost exactly on the imaginary 'Highland Line' and just qualifies as producing a Highland malt whisky. The stills are unusual in that incorporated with them is a rectifying column, which can be altered to produce different weights of whisky. The bulk of the malt whisky produced goes for blending. Since the takeover of Barton Distilling (Scotland) Ltd, by Amalgamated Distilled Products plc in 1982 the American based ownership of this distillery passed to the Glen Catrine Bonded Warehouse Ltd, a company primarily concerned with warehousing, blending and bottling whisky, but a limited amount of malt whisky is now bottled under the name **Inchmurrin**, after a prominent nearby island on Loch Lomond.

Owned by
Glen Catrine Bonded Warehouse Ltd

Visitors
By arrangement

Age and strength when bottled
No age given at 40% volume

Comments
Still quite hard to find, this is a reasonably interesting but rather light malt whisky.

LOCHNAGER *see* ROYAL LOCHNAGAR

LOCHSIDE

Situation
Lochside, Montrose, Angus. Grampian Region

Classification
Highland (Eastern)

Origins and background
Built originally in the 18th century as a brewery which it still resembles, the actual date when it was established and the names of its early owners have been forgotten. In the early 19th century it was owned by a William Ross who sold it to James Deuchar & Sons Ltd, of Newcastle on Tyne. It was later bought by Scottish & Newcastle Breweries Ltd, who shipped the beer from Montrose to Newcastle. Finally, in 1957, it was acquired by Joseph W. Hobbs who already owned the Ben Nevis distillery and was converted into a distillery capable, like Ben Nevis, of producing grain and malt whisky with a patent still alongside the pot malt stills. The company in whose name it was controlled was MacNab Distilleries Ltd. In 1973 the large Spanish Company Destilerias y Crianza del Whisky S.A. of Madrid, known as DYC for short, acquired the distillery, the first continental takeover of a distillery. They closed down the grain distillery and concentrated on producing highland malt whisky. The distillery has a capacity of a million proof gallons a year. Most of the production goes for blending in Scotland, although some goes to Italy and some to Spain for use in blended Spanish whisky. Some is also bottled by the independent distillers.

Owned by
Destilerias y Crianza del Whisky S.A., Madrid (DYC)

Visitors
By arrangement

Age and strength when bottled
Only bottled by the independent bottlers

Comments
This seems a smooth enough dry dram, which might well merit bottling by the distillery.

LOMOND

Situation
Dumbarton. Strathclyde Region

Classification
Lowland (Western)

Origins and background
In effect this is part of the Inverleven distillery since it uses
a unique type of flat-sided still invented by a Hiram Walker
employee, now dead, a Mr Fred Whiting. It takes the same
low wines and feints charger and the same spirit receiver
as Inverleven but the stills produce a whisky quite distinct
from the other, thus giving Hiram Walker the advantage
of having two separate malts from what is in essence the
same distillery complex. The malt whisky produced is all
used for blending.

Owned by
Allied Distillers Ltd

Visitors
By arrangement

Age and strength when bottled
None bottled

Comments
It would be interesting to be able to test the difference
between this and Inverleven for oneself rather than relying
on hearsay.

LONGMORN

Situation
Elgin, Morayshire. Grampian Region

Classification
Highland (Speyside)

Origins and background
Two and a half miles south of Elgin near the village of
Longmorn, with a water supply from a never-failing local
spring and peat obtained from nearby Mannoch Hill, this
distillery was built in 1897 by John Duff at the height of
the whisky boom. In the same year he also built the neigh-
bouring Benriach distillery, see Benriach. The controlling
company was John Duff & Co. Ltd, but in 1898 James R.
Grant took over Longmorn, to be succeeded by his sons
P. J. C. Grant and R. L. Grant, trading as the Longmorn
Distillery Co. The Grants of Longmorn and the Grants of
Glen Grant were finally united in 1970 when Hill Thomson
& Co. Ltd, noted whisky blenders and merchants of 45
Frederick Street, Edinburgh, where they had been trading
since 1799, and Longmorn-Glenlivet Distillers Ltd, merged
with The Glenlivet and Glen Grant Distilleries Ltd, under
the banner of The Glenlivet Distillers. (See The Glenlivet.)
Only eight years later, in 1978, they were acquired by
Seagram Distillers plc, thus ending a proud record of
independent and dedicated Scottish control.

Owned by
The Seagram Co. Ltd

Visitors
By arrangement. Tel: 05422 7471

Age and strength when bottled
15 years and 43% volume

Comments
This used to be one of the very finest malt whiskies when
bottled at 10 years and 40% volume, a fine, very pale, and
delicate flavour making it an excellent dram before or after
dinner. After being taken over by Seagram it ceased to

be bottled except for the French market. Happily it is now bottled again, but at 15 years, no doubt to fit in with Seagram's marketing policy of having different malts available covering a range of ages. It is now rather darker coloured and with the delicacy and fragrance it formerly had perhaps slightly masked by being too long in the cask. It is still however a very fine dram to drink at any time, if you can find it.

LONGROW *see* SPRINGBANK

MACALLAN

Situation
Craigellachie, Banffshire. Grampian Region

Classification
Highland (Speyside)

Origins and background
The distillery was first licensed legally on the Macallan's farm above a well known ford over the river Spey and the famous rock of Craigellachie in 1824, but there can be little doubt that illicit distilling had been carried on there for a number of years previously. This was a natural crossing on the Spey for the travelling cattle drovers who would generally spend a night at the farm, where it was reasonable that they would drink quantities of illicitly distilled whisky. They were also the obvious middle-men between the merchants in the south and the illicit distillers in the north, hence the Macallan farm was ideally placed for illicit distilling. As with The Glenlivet, the reputation of the whisky was already too widespread immediately after the legal licensing of the distillery to account for its popularity in the south in any other way. The Macallan, like The Glenlivet, was off to a head start when the 1823 Act came into being in 1824. Nevertheless the distillery changed hands several times in the course of the 19th century before James Stuart sold it to Roderick Kemp in 1892. Kemp had been trained as a distiller at Talisker and soon began to improve Macallan.

By the time Kemp died in 1909 Macallan was already regarded as one of the finest Speyside malts. On his death a trust was formed for his two married daughters and their progeny and their descendants are still prominent shareholders to this day. In 1950 a steady programme of modernisation and rebuilding was introduced over a six-year period, throughout which the distillery continued in full production. In 1959 further rebuilding work was carried out. Finally in 1964 a second distillery was built alongside the old one and came into production in 1966 as an integral unit with the old.

Production is now around the one and a half million gallon mark a year, but remains in very high demand as one of the outstanding Highland malts. It may be that the distillery's insistence on the use of small stills similar to the originals and never using caramel for colouring, but always maturing the spirit in sherry casks, and achieving a standard colouring by blending whiskies from different casks are amongst the secrets of their outstanding success. Certainly this is a classic case where Scottish distillers unhampered by transatlantic takeovers, or accounting methods, or love of standardisation and modern marketing theories have proved themselves infinitely superior by using to the full the old methods and the well tried and tested principles of pot still malt whisky distilling. The malt whisky is marketed as The Macallan.

Owned by
The Macallan Distillers Ltd

Visitors
Reception centre. Tel: 03405 471

Age and strength when bottled
10 year old at 40% volume and 57% volume; also 12 and 18 years at 43% volume and 25 years at 43% volume

Comments
If only the success of this fine malt whisky could be a lesson to those transatlantic or foreign conglomerates who now own other fine malt distilleries. In any shape and form The Macallan is a joy to drink, with an initial sweetness, but smooth body and splendid aftermath and it can only be said that as it ages it improves. It is well marketed and deservedly popular.

MACDUFF

Situation
Banff, Banffshire. Grampian Region

Classification
Highland (Speyside)

Origins and background
This distillery is of comparatively recent construction having been built near Banff in 1962 by a group including Brodie Hepburn Ltd, and Block, Grey and Block Ltd, and drawing its water for cooling from the nearby river Deveron. The original William Lawson was a Dundonian who started business as a whisky merchant and blender from 1849, but his company was never of any great consequence and remained quiescent for a lengthy period. The company was revived after the 1939-45 War in Liverpool as blenders and exporters and in 1967 was moved to Coatbridge where a bottling and blending unit was formed. In 1980 they became part of the General Beverage Corporation of Luxembourg, themselves a subsidiary company of Martini Rossi. They then bought the ten year old Macduff distillery and extended the warehouses. Capacity is now around 750,000 proof gallons. The malt whisky produced is called **Glen Deveron** and is readily available and well marketed.

Owned by
General Beverage Corporation, Luxembourg

Visitors
Reception centre. Tel: 02612 2612

Age and strength when bottled
12 years at 40% volume

Comments
A good straightforward Speyside after-dinner malt whisky, clean tasting with a dry and pleasing aftermath.

MANNOCHMORE

Situation
Elgin, Morayshire. Grampian Region

Classification
Highland (Speyside)

Origins and background
This distillery was built by John Haig & Co. Ltd in 1971 about two and a half miles south of Elgin, alongside their malt distillery at Glenlossie, but drawing its water from another source. It has a capacity of a million proof gallons, but all the production goes for blending.

Owned by
United Distillers

Visitors
By arrangement

Age and strength when bottled
None bottled

Comments
Even the neighbouring Glenlossie is only bottled by the independent bottlers. It is time perhaps that Guinness plc changed the old die-hard bottling attitudes of the DCL now that it has become their subsidiary, United Distillers plc.

MILTONDUFF

Situation
Elgin, Morayshire. Grampian Region

Classification
Highland (Speyside)

Origins and background
Close to the famed Pluscarden Abbey ruins, this distillery was built in 1824 in the year when the 1823 Licensing Act came into force. It is almost certain therefore that it was built on the site of a previously illicit distillery and its mash house is said to have been built on the old abbey brewhouse. The water from the Black Burn flowing from the peaty slopes of the Black Hill provides an ample water supply. It was established by Messrs Bain and Pearey, but was soon transferred to William Stuart. During the early 1890s a good deal of renovation and rebuilding took place and by 1896 it was capable of producing 300,000 proof gallons a year. After the whisky boom, in common with all other malt distilleries, it went through a long lean period. In 1936 Thomas Yool, then owner, sold the distillery to Hiram Walker-Gooderham & Worts, Ltd. It was subsequently modernised and enlarged so that it now has a capacity of two million proof gallons a year or over 5 million litres of alcohol. At one period another malt whisky known as **Mosstowie** was also produced from this complex, in Lomond type stills (See **Loch Lomond**) but these have now been dismantled although some of the product may still be available through the independent bottlers.

Owned by
Allied Distillers Ltd

Visitors
Reception centre. Tel: 0343 7433

Age and strength when bottled
12 years at 43% volume

Comments
A very reasonable Speyside after-dinner malt whisky, smooth and with a delicate aftermath.

MORTLACH

Situation
Dufftown, Banffshire. Grampian Region

Classification
Highland (Speyside)

Origins and background
This distillery owes its name to the parish in which it lies. The Gaelic meaning of Mortlach is 'a bowl shaped valley' and the distillery stands in a hollow in the hills just outside Dufftown on the river Dullan, but draws its water from a locally famed Priests' well. Although undoubtedly based on the site of an earlier illicit still it was first licensed in 1824 to John Findlater. In the following year he took on two partners, Gordon and Mackintosh. By 1854 Gordon was the sole survivor and was joined in that year by George Cowie. Ten years later in 1865 George Cowie was the sole owner. Trading as George Cowie & Sons the company apparently benefited from the whisky boom and was thoroughly rebuilt and renovated in 1903. After surviving the recession during the 1914-18 War it was acquired by John Walker & Sons Ltd, in 1923, thus becoming part of the DCL and now part of United Distillers plc.

Owned by
United Distillers

Visitors
By arrangement

Age and strength when bottled
12 years old and 40% volume

Comments
A mellow Speyside malt whisky making a very pleasing after-dinner dram with a good aftermath.

MOSSTOWIE *see* MILTONDUFF

NORTH PORT

Situation
Brechin, Angus. Grampian Region

Classification
Highland (Eastern)

Origins and background
A local Brechin family named Guthrie founded the North Port, or Brechin, Distillery in 1820, at which time the controlling company was the Townhead Distillery Co. The company name was changed to Guthrie, Martin & Co., and in 1893 during the whisky boom years it became a limited company. It was acquired by DCL and W. H. Holt & Co. Ltd in the lean years in 1923 and was handed over to the Scottish Malt Distillers Ltd. After 1926 the distillery was shut down for a period, but licensed to Mitchell Bros Ltd was functioning once more during the post 1939-45 War years. In 1983 it closed for the last time and dismantled.

Owned by
United Distillers

Visitors
No

Age and strength when bottled
None bottled and only available through the independent bottlers.

Comments
Some may yet be available from the independent bottlers. On one tasting it would seem a pleasant enough malt whisky but perhaps understandably was almost entirely used for blending.

OBAN

Situation
Oban, Argyll. Strathclyde Region

Classification
Highland (Western)

Origins and background
It is claimed by some that Oban is the oldest distillery
to have been in continuous production. It is said that
distilling began in 1794, since when it has had a number
of owners. In 1883 it was acquired by James Walter
Higgins. Then in 1898 it was bought by the Oban and
Aultmore Distilleries Ltd with the intention of acting as
a major supplier to the notorious Pattison Ltd, of Leith
whose bankruptcy in that year signalled the end of the
whisky boom. It was indicative of the distillery's strength
that it survived their failure and was only sold again in
1923, when a partnership bought it and formed the Oban
Distillery Co. Ltd. In 1930 the Scottish Malt Distillers Ltd
acquired the company and it became part of the DCL. It
was closed in 1968, but was opened again in 1969, barely
spoiling its claim for continuous operation.

Owned by
United Distillers

Visitors
Reception centre. Tel: 0631 62110

Age and strength when bottled
14 years at 43% volume

Comments
This is a very pleasing distinctive malt whisky with plenty
of body and a good aftermath, possibly a little more like a
Highland than West Coast dram, but equally suitable for
drinking before or after dinner.

OLD FETTERCAIRN *see* FETTERCAIRN

OLD PULTENEY *see* PULTENEY

ORD

Situation
Muir of Ord, Beauly. Highland Region

Classification
Highland (Northern)

Origins and background
The area was notorious for illicit distilling even as late as the end of the 19th century and there is little doubt that the distillery was built on the site of an old illicit still, but it was only licensed in 1838. Ample water supplies are available from Glen Oran and the Oran Burn, making illicit distilling easy. The holder of the first license was a Mr McLennan. When he died his widow married an Alexander McKenzie, who thus acquired the distillery as well. It was then acquired by John Watson & Co. Ltd, of Dundee, and finally in 1924 was bought by John Dewar just prior to their takeover by the DCL. It is notable that heather is mixed with the peat during the malt drying process and the taste of the malt probably owes something to this. Although much goes for blending it is also bottled by the distillers, but no longer marketed under the name Ord, as used to be the case. It is now sold as **Glenordie** at 12 years old.

Owned by
United Distillers

Visitors
Reception centre. Tel: 0463 870421

Age and strength when bottled
12 years old at 40% volume

Comments
A good dry and full-bodied malt whisky with a clean aftermath well worth drinking at any time.

PITTYVAICH

Situation
Dufftown, Banffshire. Grampian Region

Classification
Highland (Speyside)

Origins and background
This was built in 1974 on the outskirts of Dufftown in the Dullan Glen by Arthur Bell & Sons Ltd, close to their other distillery, named after the town. The water for the distillery is drawn from two springs Balliemore and Convalleys. It has four stills, which are exact replicas of those in its older neighbour, and it operates in conjunction with the latter as part of the same distillery complex. The entire production goes for blending and is not bottled separately. The distillery sometimes uses the Glenlivet affix, for which there is surely no justification. It is now part of United Distillers plc.

Owned by
United Distillers

Visitors
Reception centre. Tel: 0340 20561

Age and strength when bottled
None bottled

Comments
It seems a shame that a token bottling is not made even if it is presumably a malt whisky mainly suited for blending.

PORT ELLEN

Situation
Port Ellen, Islay. Argyll. Strathclyde Region

Classification
Islay (Western Isles)

Origins and background
This distillery is actually sited about half a mile outside
Port Ellen and was built in 1825. The company formed
to run the distillery was A. K. McKay & Co. who owned
it for ten years. In 1836 the company was taken over by
the MP for Stirling, John Ramsay, who was an important
figure in the Scotch whisky industry at the time. Some of
the research undertaken by Robert Stein and Aeneas Coffy
for their invention of the patent still was carried out in Port
Ellen and Ramsay was also the pioneer of the spirit safe
which HM Customs and Excise subsequently adopted. He
was succeeded by his son in 1906 who sold the distillery
in 1920 to a company called the Port Ellen Distillery Ltd.
In 1927 the distillery was acquired by John Dewar & Sons
Ltd, and so passed to the DCL. It was closed in 1930, but
re-opened in 1967 after being enlarged and modernised.
All the production was used for blending and only a little
was bottled by the independent bottlers as a malt whisky.
It is now closed once more.

Owned by
United Distillers

Visitors
By arrangement

Age and strength when bottled
Only available through the independent bottlers

Comments
Unfair as it is to make judgements on one tasting, this
seems to be a dry and typically aromatic Islay malt.

PULTENEY

Situation
Wick, Caithness. Highland Region

Classification
Highland (Northernmost)

Origins and background
Established in 1826, near the town of Wick, the distillery is not far from that notable landmark above the town, the ruined castle on the cliffs known as the Auld Man of Wick, and there are ample water supplies available, including the Loch of Hempriggs. Peat, of course, is no problem in a countryside where houses were frequently roofed with it. The lack of good road and rail communication is however indicated by the fact that this is the only distillery in Caithness and the most northerly on the mainland. The distillery remained under control of the Henderson family until the slump of the 1920s, when in 1923 it was acquired by James Watson & Co. Ltd. Like many other malt distilleries it was then closed down in 1926 during the depression years and remained closed for a long period until 1951. By then it had been acquired by Mr R. Cumming and it was bought from him in turn by Hiram Walker & Sons (Scotland) plc. They licensed it to their subsidiary J. & G. Stodart Ltd, and set about extensive renovation and modernisation. The bulk of their whisky goes for blending. It is bottled as **Old Pulteney**, but see below.

Owned by
Allied Distillers Ltd

Visitors
Reception centre. Tel: 09552 371

Age and strength when bottled
8 years old at 40% volume

Comments
This is amongst the fastest maturing of the Highland malt whiskies. It is indeed light, clean and smooth and a good pre-dinner dram, but hardly merits the prefix Old.

ROSEBANK

Situation
Camelon, Falkirk, Stirlingshire. Central Region

Classification
Lowland

Origins and background
According to the Statistical Account for Scotland of the period, Messrs Stark Brothers were distilling here in 1798, but the forerunner of the present distillery complex was begun by James Rankine in 1840 and the site was originally chosen for its ready water supplies. In 1864 he was followed by his son R. W. Rankine who rebuilt the entire distillery and increased demand for the distillery's product greatly. In 1894 the Rosebank Distillery Ltd was formed as a public company and a second issue of shares in 1897 was immediately fully subscribed. With the collapse of the whisky boom in 1900 and the slump that followed, however, Rosebank was badly hit and in 1914 was one of the companies which amalgamated to form Scottish Malt Distillers Ltd, becoming a subsidiary of the DCL and now of United Distillers plc.

Owned by
United Distillers

Visitors
By appointment. Tel: 0324-23325

Age and strength when bottled
8 and 12 years at 40% volume

Comments
A dry dram with a good flavour and plenty of body, it tastes more like a Highland than the Lowland malt whisky it undoubtedly is. The 8 year old stands up well against the older bottling, although it is naturally more mellow.

ROYAL BRACKLA

Situation
Nairn, Morayshire. Grampian Region

Classification
Highland (Northern)

Origins and background
The distillery was founded at Cawdor, close to Nairn, in 1812 by Captain William Fraser and received the prefix 'Royal' in 1835 at the command of William IV to show his approval of the whisky. Whether 'Silly Billy's' commendation was up to much is another matter, but it probably helped to sell the whisky over the years. The distillery changed hands a number of times before the Brackla Distillery Co. Ltd was formed in 1898 and acquired the lease and more land from the Earl of Cawdor for expansion. In 1919 John Mitchell and James Leith of Aberdeen acquired the company and in 1926 sold it to John Bisset & Co. Ltd of Leith. In 1943 they were taken over by DCL. Subsequently in 1965 the distillery was modernised and expanded with steam fired stills of 5,000 gallon capacity and a new malting. Almost all the production went for blending. It is now temporarily closed.

Owned by
United Distillers

Visitors
Only by arrangement

Age and strength when bottled
Only bottled by the independent bottlers

Comments
A sample 18 year old at 46% made a very good after-dinner dram with plenty of body and pleasing aftermath which suggests it should be bottled by the distillery.

ROYAL LOCHNAGAR

Situation
Crathie, Ballater, Aberdeenshire. Grampian Region

Classification
Highland (Eastern)

Origins and background
The Lochnagar distillery, only a mile from Balmoral, was built by John Begg in 1845. In 1848 on 12th September Queen Victoria accompanied by Prince Albert and her young family toured the distillery, being personally escorted by John Begg himself who persuaded them all to try a dram, for which service he duly received a royal warrant and the distillery was known for much of the 19th century as the Royal Lochnagar Distillery. The advertising slogan 'Take a peg of John Begg' was one of the earlier examples of the kind. John Begg was a considerable entrepreneur in his day and from Aberdeen initially set up a worldwide export and blending business finally based in Glasgow. On his death in 1880 his son Henry Begg took over and continued the business as John Begg. In 1916 they were taken over by DCL and the Royal prefix was dropped for some time, but has since been resuscitated. Much of the production goes for blending, but some is bottled as the only example of a Deeside malt whisky.

Owned by
United Distillers

Visitors
Reception centre. Tel 03384 273

Age and strength when bottled
12 years at 40% volume

Comments
A very pleasant smooth tasting fresh clean after-dinner dram with a good aftermath.

SCAPA

Situation
Kirkwall, Orkney

Classification
Island (Orkney)

Origins and background
In 1885 Mr J. T. Townsend, a Speyside distiller, built what was then a very advanced distillery two miles from Kirkwall, the capital of Orkney, on the north side of Scapa Flow and obtaining its water supplies from the Lingro Burn. It naturally has had very close connections during both world wars and after the First World War German Fleet was scuttled in full view of the distillery. The distillery itself had naval ratings billeted in it during the War and when fire broke out they helped to fight the blaze and save the distillery. After the War control was passed to the Scapa Distillery Co. Ltd, subsequently taken over by Bloch Brothers (Distillers) Ltd. Then in 1934 Hiram Walker & Sons (Scotland) plc acquired it as part of their plans for venturing into the industry in Scotland and it was largely rebuilt in 1959. It is licensed to one of their subsidiaries, the blending company Taylor & Ferguson Ltd, also acquired in the 1930s. It is currently shut down.

Owned by
Allied Distillers Ltd

Visitors
By arrangement. Tel: 0856 2071

Age and strength when bottled
It is only obtainable from the independent bottlers.

Comments
A dram at 8 years and 40% volume made a good after dinner drink recognisable as having a resemblance to the Orkney 'Highland Park,' which makes it sadder that this is not likely to be available.

SINGLETON *see* AUCHROISK

SPEYBURN

Situation
Rothes, Morayshire. Grampian Region

Classification
Highland (Speyside)

Origins and background
The distillery was built towards the end of the Scotch whisky boom in 1896, by the brothers John and Edward Hopkins in partnership with their cousin Edward Broughton, with whom they controlled the well-known whisky blending and marketing firm of John Hopkins & Company Ltd which dated from 1872. There is a plentiful water supply from the springs in the hills of the Glen of Rothes. After building the distillery at Rothes, it was registered in the name of the Speyburn-Glenlivet Distillery Co. Ltd, using the affix Glenlivet. In 1916 John Hopkins was taken over by DCL, but was not totally integrated until 1931. The distillery is not a large one, but it has been prominent in trying to overcome the problem of pollution in the River Spey. The entire production goes for blending and is accepted as of high quality, but a little is occasionally available from the independent bottlers.

Owned by
United Distillers

Visitors
Reception centre. Tel: 03403 213

Age and strength when bottled
Only bottled by the independent bottlers

Comments
After tasting a 16 year old at 46% volume it can only be said that this seems a full-bodied after-dinner dram which should merit bottling.

SPRINGBANK

Situation
Campbeltown, Argyll. Strathclyde Region

Classification
Campbeltown

Origins and background
Campbeltown was once regarded as the whisky capital of Scotland with something like forty distilleries in and around the town. Springbank, established by the Mitchell family in the late 1820s is one of the two remaining and the only one to have survived without closing. It is still owned by J. & A. Mitchell & Co. Ltd, the family concern, the present owners being direct descendants of the founders. An unusual feature is that a special spirit still used for the foreshots and feints instead of returning them for redistillation as is usual. One other notable feature is that it is one of the few distilleries to bottle its own malt on site. (Another is Glenfiddich) It should also be noted particularly that the distillery produces two different malt whiskies. As well as Springbank it produces another named **Longrow**. This is distilled with only peat-dried malted barley making it much heavier as a result. The distillery has three times won the Championship Award at the Wine & Spirit Fair at Ljubljana in Yugoslavia.

Owned by
J. & A. Mitchell & Co. Ltd

Visitors
By arrangement

Age and strength when bottled
12, 15, 21 and 30 years at 46% volume

Comments
Springbank is an interesting and distinctive malt whisky rather reminiscent of an Irish whiskey with an initial sweetness and a pleasing aftermath making an altogether very satisfying dram. Longrow at 14 years and 46% is more like a smooth west coast malt whisky, reminiscent of an Islay dram with a long aftermath.

STRATHISLA

Situation
Keith, Banffshire. Grampian Region

Classification
Highland (Speyside)

Origins and background
In 1786 a Mr George Taylor obtained a charter from the
Earl of Findlater and Seafield for a distillery on the site,
thus making this one of the earliest operating distilleries
in the Highlands. From around 1830 it was owned and
managed by William Longmore and his successors, initially as the Strathisla distillery and latterly as the Milton
distillery, a name still used by some locals. It was still
a private company when acquired by Chivas Brothers
Ltd, in 1950, themselves a subsidiary of Seagram Distillers
plc, who promptly changed the name back from Milton
to Strathisla and added the hyphenated Glenlivet affix,
although a considerable distance from the Livet. While
still adding the affix to their distillery name it has now
been dropped from the label on the bottle. Strathisla in
fact obtain their water supplies for cooling from the River
Isla and for distilling from a reservoir filled by a spring in
the hills. On the other side of the River Isla stands the
sister distillery, Glen Keith (another that used to add the
Glenlivet affix) which was built in 1956. Most goes for
blending but some is bottled by Chivas Brothers and the
independent bottlers.

Owned by
The Seagram Co. Ltd

Visitors
Reception centre. Tel: 05422 7471

Age and strength when bottled
12 years and 40% volume

Comments
Bottled by Chivas Brothers this malt whisky is hard to
come by but it is a pleasantly smooth medium-bodied dry
after-dinner dram.

STRATHMILL

Situation
Keith, Banffshire. Grampian Region

Classification
Highland (Speyside)

Origins and background
Originally called the Glenisla-Glenlivet Distillery, Strath-mill was built on the site of a former mill in 1891 and was acquired by W. & A. Gilbey in 1895 at the height of the Scotch whisky boom. Initially they marketed malt whisky only, but then turned to blending and marketed their noted blend Glen Spey. In 1962 they merged with Gilbey Twiss, Justerini & Brooks and United Vintners to form the International Distillers & Vintners. The output of the distillery is now all used for blending.

Owned by
International Distillers & Vintners Ltd

Visitors
By arrangement

Age and strength when bottled
None bottled by the distillery

Comments
Some is available from time to time through the independent bottlers.

TALISKER

Situation
Carbost, Isle of Skye

Classification
Island (Skye)

Origins and background
First established in 1830 the distillery was twice moved
before settling where it now sited on the shores of Loch
Harport. Its water for distilling is obtained from the nearby
Carbost Burn. In 1898 the Talisker Distillery Ltd, amalgamated with the Dailuane-Glenlivet Distillery Ltd, which
resulted in the formation of Dailuane-Talisker Distilleries
Ltd, which also controlled the Imperial-Glenlivet Distillery
close to Dailuane. The three distilleries in this group were
acquired in 1916 jointly by Dewar, DCL, W. P. Lowrie and
Johnnie Walker. In 1925 at the time of the great amalgama-
tion which saw Dewar and John Walker both absorbed into
DCL they also became part of DCL and since then have
been controlled by Scottish Malt Distillers, although for
many years the three were run as a separate company.

Owned by
United Distillers

Visitors
Reception centre. Tel: 047842 203

Age and strength when bottled
10 years at 45.8% volume

Comments
A very smooth and pleasing distinctive and unmistakeably
west coast malt whisky with a full body and strong aftermath making a notable after-dinner dram.

TAMDHU *(tamdoo)*

Situation
Kockando, Morayshire. Grampian Region

Classification
Highland (Speyside)

Origins and background
Yet another of the many distilleries built around the time of the Scotch whisky boom years this distillery was established in 1897. The Gaelic meaning of Tamdhu is 'small black hill' and it is under just such a hill that the distillery lies on the banks of the Spey. In 1898 the controlling company Tamdhu-Glenlivet Ltd was acquired by The Highland Distilleries Co. Ltd, although operating as a separate subsidiary. In common with many others the distillery was shut down for a long period from 1927 to 1948, but, renovated and modernised, it forms an important part of the group. It is now readily available bottled by the distillers.

Owned by
The Highland Distilleries Co. plc

Visitors
Reception centre. Tel: 03406 221

Age and strength when bottled
10 years at 40% volume

Comments
A sound, full-bodied malt whisky with a good mellow aftermath making a pleasing after-dinner dram. It is well marketed and readily obtainable.

TAMNAVULIN–GLENLIVET

(tamnavoolin)

Situation
Ballindalloch, Banffshire. Grampian Region

Classification
Highland (Speyside)

Origins and background
The Gaelic meaning of Tamnavulin is 'the mill on the hill' and near to the site of this distillery are the ruins of an old mill. It was built by the Invergordon Distillers Ltd in 1966 on the west bank of the river Livet at the base of the Cairngorm mountains. It is among the few distilleries which is entitled to use the hyphenated affix Glenlivet with good reason. Although a good deal undoubtedly is used in the many Invergordon blends it is also bottled as a malt whisky.

Owned by
Invergordon Distillers Ltd

Visitors
Reception centre with a picnic area. Tel: 08073 442

Age and strength when bottled
10 years at 40% volume

Comments
A light, slightly peaty, typical smooth Speyside malt whisky with a good aftermath making a pleasing dram at any time.

TEANINICH

Situation
Alness, Ross-shire. Highland Region

Classification
Highland (Northern)

Origins and background
Facing the Cromarty Firth this distillery probably dates back to the 18th century. Some of the original buildings put up by Captain H. Munro of Teaninich in 1817 are still visible today. The distillery is close to the River Averon from which its water supplies are obtained. The Teaninich Munros, a branch of the Munros of Foulis, gave up distilling in the 1850s when they let the premises to successive tenants. In 1895 two partners named Munro and Cameron took over the distillery and acquired the lease from the Munro family. In 1905 on his partner's death Robert Innes Cameron took over the entire operation. In 1933 his trustees sold out to the DCL. The entire production went for blending, but the distillery has been closed for some years.

Owned by
United Distillers

Visitors
By arrangement

Age and strength when bottled
Not bottled by the distillers

Comments
On a sample bottled at 26 years and 46% volume by the independent bottlers this seems a very smooth dry after-dinner dram.

TOBERMORY

Situation
Tobermory, Mull, Argyll.

Classification
Island (Mull)

Origins and background
The distillery dates back to the start of the 18th century when there was undoubtedly a good deal of illicit distilling on the island. After its foundation it had a number of owners until bought by John Hopkins & Co. Ltd, around 1890. When the company was taken over in 1916 the distillery became part of the DCL. It was shut down in 1928 because of the financial situation and was used as an electricity generating station. In 1972 a Liverpool Shipping Company financed a complete rebuilding and re-equipping of the distillery, with assistance from Spanish and Panamanian backers, and formed a company called the Ledaig Distillery (Tobermory) Ltd, and it was then bottled as Ledaig. By 1975 the company closed down having just raised the distillery's capacity to 800,000 gallons a year. In 1976 a Receiver was appointed, but in 1979 the Kirkleavington Property Co. took over the company from the bank and started operating again as the Tobermory Distillers Ltd. The bulk of the production went for blending, but it was also available as a malt whisky. Unfortunately it closed again in 1981 and subsequently is hard to find.

Owned by
Kirkleavington Property Co.

Visitors
By arrangement

Age and strength when bottled
No age given at 40% volume

Comments
A dry and peaty interesting malt whisky more like a Speyside product than a west coast island dram. Occasionally available from the independent bottlers.

TOMATIN

Situation
Tomatin, Inverness-shire. Highland Region

Classification
Highland (Northern)

Origins and background
About thirteen miles south-east of Inverness and built around the 1,028 foot level this distillery is remote enough, although within easy reach of the main road and the railway. Established in 1897 it survived the succeeding years well and up to the outbreak of the Second World War was eminently successful. On resuming distilling after the War the distillery was producing 120,000 proof gallons from its two pot stills a year. After successive programmes of modernisation the number of stills was increased to 23 with a capacity of 5 million proof gallons by 1975.

A high degree of automation and the latest methods were introduced throughout the entire distilling process, so that only a small workforce was required, despite the size of the operation. Water for the distilling process is obtained from the Monadhliaith Mountains via a local burn the Alt-na-Frithe, which flows into the River Findhorn not far away. After a series of financial upsets the company was forced to close the distillery temporarily and was finally acquired by the Japanese company Takara Shuzo & Okura, the first whisky distillery to be taken over by Japanese interests. Most goes for blending but it is also exported in bulk and a good deal goes for export, nevertheless it is also available as a malt whisky.

Owned by
Takara Shuzo & Okura & Co. Ltd

Visitors
Reception centre. Tel: 08082 234

Age and strength when bottled
10 years at 40% volume

Comments
A medium smooth, fairly bland, pre-dinner dram.

TOMINTOUL–GLENLIVET *(tomintowl)*

Situation
Ballindalloch, Banffshire. Grampian Region

Classification
Highland (Speyside)

Origins and background
This modern distillery was established in 1965 by two
firms of Glasgow whisky brokers, Hay & MacLeod &
Co. and W. & S. Strong & Co., because of the shortage
of malt whisky available for blending at that time. They
chose a site some five miles north of Tomintoul close to
the Glenlivet area with a plentiful supply of water from
the Ballantruan Spring. Later additions brought the total
capacity up to a million proof gallons, or 2.52 million
litres of alcohol, a year with storage on the spot for two
and a half million gallons, or 6.3 million litres of alcohol.
The founder firms of whisky brokers subsequently merged
with Whyte & Mackay Ltd. Most of the production goes
into Whyte & Mackay blends, but some is bottled and the
Glenlivet affix is justified.

Owned by
Whyte & Mackay Distillers Ltd

Visitors
Reception centre. Tel: 08073 274

Age and strength when bottled
10 years at 40% volume

Comments
A very light and smooth pre-dinner dram with a good
aftermath.

TORMORE

Situation
Advie, Grantown-on-Spey. Grampian Region

Classification
Highland (Speyside)

Origins and background
Built in 1959 by Seager Evans & Co. Ltd this was the first completely new distillery to be built on Speyside this century. It was built to a totally new design by a past President of the Royal Academy, Sir Albert Richardson. It was a complete breakaway from traditional designs and consists of a distillery, warehouses and cooperage, as well as houses for the distillery workers, all built in Kemnay granite. Ample water supplies are available from the nearby Loch an Oir, which in Gaelic means Loch of Gold. Much of the product is used for blending but some is bottled for the distillery, now acquired from Long John International Ltd, by Allied Distillers Ltd.

Owned by
Allied Distillers Ltd

Visitors
Welcome by arrangement

Age and strength when bottled
10 years at 40% volume

Comments
A medium and fairly typically Speyside malt whisky with a pleasant aftermath making a satisfactory if rather light pre-dinner dram. It is also bottled as a 5 year old at 43% volume but for export only. This is, however, generally obtainable at airports in the duty-free shops and is also a good dram.

TULLIBARDINE *(tullibardeen)*

Situation
Blackford, Perthshire. Highland Region

Classification
Highland (Southern)

Origins and background
The distillery stands on the site of a 17th century Blackford
Brewery in a hollow beneath the Ochil hills and takes
its name from the moor of Tullibardine on which the
nearby Gleneagles Hotel was built. The plentiful supplies
of particularly good water for brewing ale for which the
old brewery at Blackford was noted are now utilised
by the distillery. The distillery was designed by Mr W.
Delme Evans in 1949 for Wm S. Scott Ltd, but was
acquired by Brodie Hepburn Ltd, and subsequently sold to
Invergordon Distillers Ltd, in 1972. Two years later in 1974
after considerable rebuilding the distillery's capacity was
doubled. Most is used for blending, but it is also bottled
by the distillery. In such a convenient position adjacent
to a much visited golf and tourist centre it has naturally
become well geared to visitors.

Owned by
Invergordon Distillers Ltd

Visitors
Reception centre. Tel: 076482 252

Age and strength when bottled
10 years at 40% volume

Comments
This is light, fresh and clean, more resembling a Lowland
malt whisky perhaps, but with a good aftermath and
making a pleasant pre-dinner dram.

Recent Closures

In recent years the following distilleries have irrevocably closed, but occasional bottles mat still be available from time to time through independent bottlings.

Banff (Banff, Banffshire. Grampian Region)
Closed in 1983 and demolished by United Distillers.
Benromach (Forres, Morayshire. Grampian Region)
Dismantled in the 1980s by United Distillers.
Dallas Dhu (2 miles south of Forres. Grampian Region)
Closed by United distillers in 1983 and reopened as a museum showing the workings of a traditional distillery.
Glen Albyn (Inverness. Highland Region)
Closed by United Distillers in 1983 and since demolished.
Glen Mhor (Inverness. Highland Region)
Next to above and also demolished by United Distillers.
Glenugie (Peterhead, Aberdeenshire. Grampian Region)
The most easterly distillery it was closed by Long John International in 1982 and the machinery sold for scrap.
Kinclaith (Near Glasgow. Strathclyde Region)
In operation for only 18 years, the distillery was dismantled in 1975 by Long John International.
Millburn (Inverness. Highland Region)
Closed and dismantled in 1985 by United Distillers the site is now occupied by a restaurant.
St Magdalene (Linlithgow, West Lothian. Lothian Region)
Closed down in 1983 by United Distillers, the site was developed into flats.

An Almanack of Distilling Dates and Events

800 B.C.	Arrack known to have been distilled in India.
584 B.C.	Aristotle born; later wrote of distilling in his *Meteorology*.
A.D. 432	St Patrick, a native of Scotland, sent to Wicklow to spread Christianity and also reputed to have introduced distilling.
1494	Entry in Exchequer Rolls regarding Friar Cor making aqua vitae by order of the King.
1498	Lord High Treasurer's Account 'To the barbour that brocht aqua vitae to the King in Dundee.'
1505	Barber surgeons in Edinburgh granted right of making aqua vitae.
1506	Treasurer's accounts in Inverness mention 'aqua vite to the King.'
1527	*The vertuose boke of Distyllacyon* by Hieronymous Braunschweig published in English, translated by L. Andrew. First book on the subject, treated aqua vitae as a medicine.
1559	*Treasures of Evonymous* published by Peter Morwyng detailed methods of distilling process.
1579	First Act in Scotland specifically relating to Aqua Vitae.
1618	John Taylor in his *Pennyless Pilgrimage* visits the Earl of Mar and drinks aqua vitae. Earliest reference to 'uisge' being drunk at a Highland chieftain's funeral.
1644	Charles I passed an Act of Excyse on 'everie pynt of aquavytie or strongh watteris sold within the country.'
1655	R. Hage accused of distilling on the Sabbath in St Ninian's Kirk session records.
1675	Boyle re-discovered the principle of the hydrometer.
1690	Ferintosh first distillery mentioned by name. Forbes of Culloden who had 'suffered the loss of his brewery of aqua vitae by fire in his absence' in 1689 fighting for William of Orange against James was granted freedom from excise duty.

1707	Act of Union of Parliaments passed against much opposition, specifically excluded a tax on malt in Scotland.
1715	Attempt to introduce Malt Tax in Scotland withdrawn.
1725	Malt taxed in Scotland and riots resulted.
1726	In his *Letters* Captain Burt, an English engineer in the Highlands referred to the Highlanders drinking whisky 'like water.'
1736	Gin Act in England aimed at checking consumption caused open flouting of Law at height of Gin Era.
1745	Prince Charles raised standard at Glenfinnan.
1746	Prince Charles defeated at Culloden and fled country.
1747	Lt. Col. Watson in Fort Augustus advised his officers to get the Highlanders 'drunk with whisky.'
1751	An Act of Parliament specifically ended Scotland's exemption from taxation so that it was no longer advantageous to import spirits from Scotland.
1784	The Wash Act defined the Highland Line by Act of Parliament.
1786	Distillery Act introduced Licensing system at prompting of English gin lobby. Duty raised in Scotland to English level. No distinction between Highlands and Lowlands. This unfairness resulted in much illicit distilling.
1788	Duty increased. Stein brothers bankrupted.
1793	Tax on whisky trebled to £9
1795	Tax on whisky doubled to £18. Some stills operated continuously to beat tax.
1797	Tax trebled to £54
1800	Tax doubled again to £108
1805	Tax raised yet again to £162. The firm of Seager Evans was formed in London to make gin.
1814	Stills under 500 gallons forbidden in the Highlands, which General Stewart of Garth said amounted to a complete interdict. Matthew Gloag set up as a whisky merchant in Perth.
1815	The output of the distillery at Drumin in Glenlivet run by George Smith grandson of John Smith Gow was already a hogshead a week. Due to the pure water and fine peat available the illicit whisky distilled there was regarded as the finest in Scotland and

was drunk by many Highland lairds including Grant of Rothiemurchus, MP and lawyer in Edinburgh.

1817 Teaninich distillery built by Captain H. Munro in Rossshire.

1818 Bladnoch distillery founded near Wigtown by the Maclelland family.

1819 Clynelish distillery near Brora built by Marquis of Stafford.

1820 John Walker set up as a licensed grocer in Kilmarnock.

1821 Linkwood distillery near Elgin was built.

1822 George IV visited Scotland and was provided with illicitly distilled Glenlivet whisky from Grant of Rothiemurchus.

1823 A new Act introduced a £10 License fee and duty of 2s 3d per gallon of whisky distilled.
Springbank distillery near Campbeltown founded by farmers named Mitchell.

1824 At the prompting of his landlord, the Duke of Gordon, George Smith took out the first license under the new Act as the first legal distillery in Glenlivet.

1825 T. R. Sandeman started as a whisky merchant in Perth.

1826 Robert Stein patented his single-distillation still.
Tax raised to 2s 10d per proof gallon.

1830 Tax per proof gallon raised to 3s 6d.
Stein built his first patent-still at Kirkliston.
Talisker was founded on the Isle of Skye.

1831 Aeneas Coffey invented his patent-still making grain whisky by continuous distillation.
Justerini and Brooks went into partnership in London.

1832 The Glen Scotia distillery was founded in Campbeltown by Stewart Galbraith.

1836 The Glenfarclas distillery was founded by Robert Hay.

1838 Hill Thomson whisky merchants granted Royal Warrant.

1840 Glen Grant distillery built at Rothes by James and John Grant.
Glenkinchie distillery founded in E. Lothian by J. Gray.
Tax per proof gallon raised to 3s 8d.

1841 James Chivas started as merchant in Aberdeen.

1842 Glenmorangie distillery started at Tain by William Mathieson.

1846	John Dewar started as wine and spirit merchant in Perth.
1848	Queen Victoria and family visited John Begg at Lochnagar distillery.
1853	Andrew Usher credited with producing the first blended whisky.
	Gladstone raised the tax to 4s 8d per proof gallon.
1854	Crimean war. Tax raised to 6s per proof gallon.
1855	Tax raised to 8s per proof gallon.
1856	First Trade Arrangement by Grain Distillers.
	Tax raised by 1d per proof gallon.
1857	W. & A. Gilbey set up as wine and spirit merchants. William Thomson joined William Hill and formed Hill Thomson as whisky merchants at 45 Frederick Street, Edinburgh.
1860	Gladstone raised the tax to 10s per proof gallon.
1865	Glenfarclas distillery bought by John Grant of Blairfindy.
	Whisky merchants Menzies, Barnard & Craig, John Bald & Co., John Haig & Co., NacNab Bros, Robert Mowbray and Macfarlane & Co., formed their first Trade Arrangement.
1870	*Phylloxera Vastatrix* began to attack the French vineyards.
1874	The North of Scotland Malt Distillers Association was formed.
1877	The Distillers Company Ltd was formed by the whisky merchants who had formed a Trade Arrangement in 1865 with Menzies, Barnard & Craig replaced by Stewart & Co.
	John Haig founded his company at Markinch in Fife.
1880	John Walker opened a London office.
	Colonel John Gordon Smith, son of George Smith, went to court on the subject of the use of the name Glenlivet. It was held that he was the only one entitled to the name 'The Glenlivet' everyone else had to use it as an affix to their own distillery name.
1881	Bruichladdich Islay Malt distillery was founded.
1882	William Sanderson produced his blend 'Vat 69'. James Whyte and Charles Mackay founded Whyte & Mackay Ltd.
1884	James Buchanan set up in London with the blend 'Black & White'.
	William Shaw at Hill Thomson produced the blend 'Queen Anne'.

1886	DCL shares quoted on London Stock Exchange.
1887	The Glenfiddich distillery built by William Grant. The Dufftown-Glenlivet distillery founded. Highland Distilleries was formed to acquire the Islay distillery of William Grant and the Glenrothes-Glenlivet distillery.
1888	The North British grain distillery founded with a productive capacity of 3 million gallons per annum in opposition to the growing power of the DCL. Mackie & Co., took over the Lagavulin distillery on Islay for White Horse.
1891	Balvenie distillery founded by William Grant of Glenfiddich.
1893	Cardow was bought by John Walker.
1894	Longmorn-Glenlivet was built by Longmorn Co.
1895	Aultore was built by Alexander Edward of Sanquhar, Forres.
1896	John Dewar built a distillery at Aberfeldy.
1898	The Pattison brothers went bankrupt ending the whisky boom.
1900	The tax per proof gallon was raised to 11s.
1906	Islington Borough Council brought the 'What is whisky?' case. Basically malt v. grain. DCL pressed for Royal Commission when verdict in favour of malt.
1908	A Royal Commission on Whisky decided grain and malt blended made Scotch whisky.
1909	Lloyd George raised the tax per proof gallon to 14s 9d.
1914	First World War. Scottish Malt Distillers formed as DCL subsidiary.
1915	Central Liquor Control Board formed. Immature Spirits Act required 2 years compulsory bonding.
1916	Compulsory bonding extended to 3 years.
1917	Dilution of Proof to 30 under proof. Whisky Association formed.
1918	War ended. Bonar Law increased tax by 15s 3d to 30s.
1919	Chamberlain increased tax per proof gallon to 50s.
1920	Prohibition introduced in U.S.A. Chamberlain increased tax to 72s 6d per proof gallon.
1924	John Haig merged with DCL.
1925	Buchanan-Dewars and John Walker merged with DCL with William Ross of DCL as Chairman.

1926   The Pot-Still Malt Distillers Association was formed
        in place of the North of Scotland Malt Distillers As-
        sociation to include all malt distillers.

1927   Seager Evans set up Strathclyde distillery for grain
        whisky.
        White Horse Distillers was acquired by the DCL.

1928   The Distillers Co. of Canada took over Seagrams
        and Sons.

1929   Wall Street crash and depression.

1930   Hiram Walker of Ontario acquired Glenburgie-
        Glenlivet.

1932   Prohibition repealed by President F. D. Roosevelt.

1933   Arthur Bell & Sons acquired the Blair-Athol and
        Dufftown-Glenlivet distilleries.

1936   Edward VIII abdicated. George VI succeeded. Hiram
        Walker acquired George Ballantine & Co., of Dumbar-
        ton, also Milton-Duff distillery.
        Arthur Bell & Sons acquired the Inchgower distillery
        near Fochabers.
        Seager Evans acquired John Long.

1937   Seager Evans took over Glenugie distillery at Peter-
        head.

1938   Hiram Walker opened a £3 million grain distillery at
        Inverleven, Dumbarton.

1939   Second World War.
        Tax per proof gallon raised by 10s to 82s 6d.
        Grain distilling halted, limited pot-still malt distilling
        permitted.

1940   Tax per proof gallon raised by 15s to 97s 6d.

1942   Tax per proof gallon raised by 40s to 137s 6d.

1945   End of 1939-45 War.

1947   Tax raised by 33s 4d to 190s 10d by Hugh Dalton.

1948   Tax raised by 20s to 210s 10d by Stafford Cripps.

1950   Seagrams took over Strathisla distillery.

1952   George IV succeeded by Elizabeth II.
        George & J. G. Smith Ltd, and J. & J. Grant Glen
        Grant Ltd, formed The Glenlivet & Glen Grant Dis-
        tillers Ltd.

1954   Hiram Walker took over Glencadam distillery in
        Brechin and Scapa distillery in Orkney.

1955   Hiram Walker took over Pulteney distillery in Wick.

1956   Seager Evans were bought by Schenley Industries
        of New York, in turn owned by the Glen Alden
        Corporation.

1957   Seager Evans built Kinclaith distillery near Glasgow.

1958   Seager Evans built a new distillery at Tormore on the Spey, north of Grantown-on-Spey.

1959   Inver House, an American-owned Company, a subsidiary of Publicker Industries, Inc., built a new grain distillery by Airdrie and an associated Lowland malt distillery named Glenflagler.

1960   The Scotch Whisky Association was incorporated to provide legal status in foreign courts.
       Glenfarclas distillery was doubled in size.
       Ledaig distillery was founded in Tobermory.
       Jura distillery started by Scottish & Newcastle Breweries, Ltd.

1961   The tax per proof gallon raised by 21s to 231s 10d.

1962   Seager Evans acquired Laphroaig.
       W & A Gilbey, Gilbey Twiss, Justerini & Brooks and United Vintners formed International Distillers and Vintners Ltd.

1964   The tax per proof gallon was raised to £12.87.

1965   The tax per proof gallon was raised to £14.60.
       Caperdonich and Benriach distilleries were rebuilt after having been silent for over sixty years.
       Invergordon Distillers Ltd was formed.

1966   The tax per proof gallon was raised to £16.06.
       Tamnavulin-Glenlivet distillery built by Invergordon Distillers Ltd, on the banks of the river Livet.

1968   The tax per proof gallon was raised to £17.14 in March and to £18.85 in November.

1969   Glen Alden Corporation, who owned Schenley Industries, who owned Seager Evans was taken over by Rapid American Incorporated. The name Seager Evans was changed to Long John International Ltd.

1970   The Glenlivet & Glen Grant Distilleries Ltd merged with Hill Thomson & Co. Ltd, and Longmorn-Glenlivet Distilleries Ltd.
       Amalgamated Distilled Products Ltd was formed with the Campbeltown Glen Scotia distillery and other interests.
       The Highland Distillers Co. Ltd acquired Matthew Gloag Ltd.

1971   Chivas Bros, the Scots subsidiary of Seagrams, began plans for a distillery in Glenlivet.
       Currency was decimalised in Britain.

1972   The Glenlivet & Glen Grant Distilleries Ltd rationalised their name to The Glenlivet Distillers Ltd.
       The Pot-Still Malt Distillers Association of Scotland

rationalised their name to The Malt Distillers Association of Scotland.

Watney, Mann & Co. Ltd acquired International Distillers & Vintners Ltd.

Whyte & Mackay Distillers Ltd, Dalmore and Tomintoul distilleries acquired by Scottish & Universal Investments Ltd.

1973   Britain entered the European Economic Community. With the introduction of VAT the duty on whisky was reduced for the first time since 1896.

Bladnoch distillery sold by Inver House Distillers to Arthur Bell & Sons.

Grand Metropolitan acquired Watney, Mann & Co. Ltd, hence also International Distillers & Vintners Ltd.

Braes of Glenlivet distillery started operations.

1974   The Glenlivet Distillers Ltd celebrated their 150th anniversary since George Smith first took out a licence in 1824.

The Malt Distillers of Scotland celebrated their centenary.

Lonrho acquired Scottish & Universal Investments Ltd, hence also Whyte & Mackay Distillers Ltd.

Pernod Ricard acquired House of Campbell and control of Aberlour distillery.

1975   Whitbread acquired Long John International.

Allt-a-Bhainne distillery started production for Seagram Distillers Ltd.

1976   Seagram Distillers Ltd opened a vatting and blending complex at Keith with a capacity of three and a half million gallons per annum.

1978   Seagram Distillers Ltd acquired The Glenlivet Distillers, Ltd.

1980   Heineken acquired 20% of Tomatin Distillers plc.

1981   Ben Nevis Distillery acquired by Long John International.

1982   Pernod Ricard acquired William Whiteley and control of Edradour distillery.

1983   DCL closed 11 of their 45 distilleries, including Banff, Benromach, Brora, Dallas Dhu, Glen Albyn, Glenochy, Glen Mohr, North Port, Knockdhu, Port Ellen, and St Magdalene. Banff, Glen Mohr and Glen Albyn in Inverness were subsequently demolished. Dallas Dhu re-opened in 1988 as a museum. St Magdalene in Linlithgow has been turned into flats.

1985   Invergordon Distillers acquired Mackinlay and con-
        trol of Jura and Glenallachie distilleries from Scottish
        & Newcastle Breweries.
        Glenugie Distillery dismantled and sold by Whit-
        bread.
1986   Arthur Bell & Sons plc acquired by Guinness plc after
        lengthy take-over battle.
1987   Tomatin distillery acquired by a Japanese consor-
        tium, Takara Shuzo & Okura & Co. Ltd.
        Guinness plc acquires control of DCL after allegedly
        fraudulent transactions in bitter take-over battle. It is
        agreed that HQ will be based in Scotland.
        Long John International re-named James Burroughs
        Distillers
1988   The Nikka Company of Japan acquired Ben Nevis
        Distillery from Long John International and planning
        to restart distilling in 1990.
        Management buy-out at Invergordon Distillers.
        Allied-Lyons plc acquired Hiram Walker and Allied-
        Distillers Ltd was formed, including George Ballan-
        tine & Son, William Teacher & Sons and Stewart &
        Son of Dundee.
        Whyte & Mackay sold by Lonrho to Brent Walker.
        DCL is merged with Arthur Bell & Sons plc, and is
        re-named United Distillers plc. The Headquarters to
        remain in London despite repeated assurances to the
        contrary during takeover and subsequently.
1989   Suntory holding in Macallan raised to 12%.
        Remy Martin own 11% in Macallan.
        Ardbeg distillery re-opened by Allied Distillers and
        Imperial and Glentauchers acquired from United Dis-
        tillers plc, to be re-opened.
        Management buy-out at Morrison Bowmore Distillers,
        owners of Bowmore, Auchentoshan and Glengarioch
        distilleries. Suntory has 35% holding.
        The Scotch Whisky Heritage Centre opened in
        Castlehill, Edinburgh, with superb audio-visual dis-
        plays, showing the history of Scotch whisky from
        the earliest days and the various stages of the whisky
        distilling process.
1990   Whitbread, owners of Long John International Ltd,
        James Burroughs Distillers, sell Tormore and Laph-
        roaig distilleries to Allied Distillers Ltd.
        Seagram Distillers Ltd, sell 45 Frederick Street,
        Edinburgh, the group headquarters in Edinburgh

and Hill Thomson HQ since 1857, one hundred and thirty three years after it was established as their base.

Whyte & Mackay taken over by Gallaghers Tobacco plc.

In his first budget chancellor John Major raised the tax on Scotch Whisky by 50p to £19.35 per proof gallon.

1992   European Economic Commission standards accepted. It has already decreed that Scotch whisky shall only be distilled and produced in Scotland. It must also be no less than 40% volume since at anything less it is impossible to check whether it has been distilled in Scotland.

Glossary

Diastase
: In the process of germination the embryo of the barley secretes diastase, which makes the starch in the barley soluble and breaks it down. This is then checked by drying.

Draff
: The grain left in the mash tun after the wort has been drawn off for distilling. It is widely used as cattle food and is one of the by-products of the distilling process.

Drying shed
: With its typical pagoda-shaped ventilators the drying shed, where the malted barley is dried, is one of the established features of the older distilleries in Scotland.

Feints
: This is the third part of the distilled spirit in the second distillation of the pot-still distilling process. It consists of the undesirable higher alcohols. They are generally re-distilled.

Foreshots
: These are the first part of the distilled spirit in the second distillation of the pot-still distilling process. They consist of the undesirable lower alcohols. The 'middle cut' which follows is the desirable spirit used to make malt whisky.

Highland Line
: Introduced by Act of Parliament in 1784 to define for tax purposes the difference between Highland and Lowland distillers. If the line were applicable today most of the Banffshire and Aberdeen distilleries would be considered Lowland.

Low Wines
: This is the product of the first part of the pot-still distilling process. It is the product of the distilled wash. The feints and foreshots are generally added to this prior to the second distilling process.

Mash
: The dried malted barley is ground in a mill and then mixed with boiling water in a circular container known as the mash tun. The soluble starch is then turned into a sugary liquid called wort.

Middle cut
: The desirable spirit produced between the foreshots and the feints in the pot-still process.

Patent still
: Also known as the Coffey Still, after its inventor

	Aeneas Coffey. Also known as a continuous still, since it works continuously producing grain whisky, unlike the two separate operations of the pot-still.
Pot still	A large, usually round-sided, copper vessel used for the distillation of malt whisky. There are two pot stills required for the process. Firstly the wash still which produces low wines. These are then distilled in the adjoining smaller spirit still which produces malt whisky.
Proof	This is the technical term by which the strength of the spirit produced is measured. One of the early methods used was to mix the spirit with gunpowder and light it. If the powder lit there was deemed to be enough spirit to allow it to do so and this was then known as 'proved'. If there was no flash the spirit was held to be too weak. Today using a Sikes Hydrometer the strength is accurately measured.
Proof Spirit	Under the 1952 Customs & Excise Act 'Spirits shall be deemed to be at proof if the volume of the ethyl alcohol contained therein made up to the volume of the spirits with distilled water has a weight equal to that of twelve-thirteenths of a volume of distilled water equal to the volume of the spirits, the volume of each liquid being computed as at 51 degrees Fahrenheit.'
Saccharify	To convert into sugar. In the distilling process this arises between malting and mash tun when the diastase enzyme turns the starch in the grain into sugar.
Single whisky	Either malt or grain whisky produced by a single distillery.
Single-single	Either malt or grain whisky produced from a single distillation by a single distillery.
Uisge Beatha	The Gaelic for *eau de vie* or water of life. Used to refer to spirit distilled from malted barley it was shortened to 'uisge,' or 'usky,' hence the origin of the word whisky.
Wash	The term used for the liquid obtained from fermented wort. This is used for the first pot-still distillation process or for the patent still.
Wort	The liquid drawn from the mash tun containing

the sugar from the malted barley. With the addition of yeast it is then fermented prior to being distilled as wash.

Zern, a   A Transatlantic term for a measure of Scotch malt whisky; a sufficient quantity taken after any sporting activity to repel any chill and induce reflective discussion of the day; hence, a Zernful.

Further Reading

Bell, Colin: *Scotch Whisky* (Lang Syne Publishers 1954)
Barnard, Alfred: *The Whisky Distilleries of the United Kingdom*: (Harper 1887)
Brander, Michael: *The Original Scotch* (Hutchinson, London 1974) *A Guide to Scotch Whisky* (Johnston & Bacon 1975) *An Introduction to Scotch Whisky* (Spurbooks 1982)
Bruce-Lockhart, Sir Robert: *Scotch* (Putnam, 1959)
Cooper, Derek: *A Taste of Scotch* (Deutsch 1989) *A Guide to the Whiskies of Scotland* (Pitman, 1981) *The Century Companion to Whiskies* (Century, 1987) & Fay Godwin: *The Whisky Roads of Scotland* (Norman & Hobhouse, 1982) & Dione Patullo: *Enjoying Scotch* (Cassel, 1980)
Daiches, David: *Scotch Whisky: Past & Present* (Collins) *Scotch Whisky* (Deutsch, 1969) *Let's Collect Scotch Whisky* (Jarrold)
Dunnett, Alastair: *The Land of Scotch* (S.W.A, 1953)
Fleming, Susan: *The Little Whisky Book* (Piatkus)
Gunn, Neil. M: *Whisky and Scotland* (Routledge, 1935)
Hallgarten, Peter: *Spirits & Liqueurs* (Faber & Faber, 1979)
Hastings, Derek: *Spirits and Liqueurs of the World* (Apple:,1984)
House, Jack: *The Pride of Perth: A History of Arthur Bell & Sons* (Hutchinson Benham, 1976) with Theodora FitzGibbon, S. Russell Grant, Donald Mackinlay, High MacDiarmid, Bill Simpson & Anthony Troon: *Scotch Whisky* (Macmillan, 1979)
Hume, James R: See Moss:
Jackson, Michael: *Malt Whisky* (Dorling Kindersley, 1989) *The World Guide to Whisky* (Dorling Kindersley) *A Guide to Scotch Whisky* (1988)
Keegan, Alan: *Scotch in Miniature*: (Famedrame, 1976)
Lamond, John: *Scotland's Malt Distilleries* (Benedict Books, 1989)
Laver, James: *The House of Haig* (1958)
Lord, Tony: *The World Guide to Spirits, Liqueurs, Aperitifs and Cocktails* (Macdonald & Janes, 1979)
MacDonald, Aeneas: *Whisky* (Porpoise Press, 1950)
Mackie, Albert D: *The Scotch Whisky Drinker's Companion* (Ramsay Head Press, 1975)
McDowall, R. J. S: *The Whiskies of Scotland* (John Murray, 1967)
Milroy, Wallace: *Malt Whisky Almanac* (Lochar, 1986)
Morrice, Philip: *The Schweppes Guide to Scotch* (Alphabooks, 1983) *The Whisky Distilleries of Scotland and Ireland* (Harper)

Moss, Michael S. & James R. Hume: *The Making of Scotch Whisky* (James & James)

Murphy, Brian: *The World Book of Whisky* (Collins, 1978)

Robb, J. Marshall: *Scotch Whisky* (W & R Chambers, 1950)

Ross, James: *Whisky* (Routledge, 1970)

Saintsbury, George : *Notes on a Cellar Book* (Macmillan, 1920)

Sillett, S. W: *Illicit Scotch* (Beaver Books, 1965)

Simon, Andre: *Drink* (Burke Publishing, 1948)

Skipton, Mark: *The Scotch Whisky Book* (Hamlyn, 1980)

Stenekey, Fred: *Whisky: The Complete Whisky Book* (1980)

Targett, David and Raymond K. Ashton: *Scotch Whisky: Too Much or too Little* (Tomatin Distillers, Co., Ltd., 1981)

Taylor, Iain Cameron: *Highland Whisky:* (An Comunn Caidhealach, 1968)

Weir, Ronald B: *A History of the Pot Still Malt Distillers' Association* (Elgin, 1970)

Wilson, John: *Scotland's Malt Whiskies* (Famedrame, 1975) *Scotland's Distilleries: A Visitor's Guide* (Famedrame)

Wilson, Neil: *Scotch & Water* (Lochar Publishing)

Wilson, Ross: *Scotch Made Easy* (Hutchinson, 1959) *Scotch* (Constable, 1970) *Scotch, Its History and Romance* (David & Charles, 1973)